When you're ready to take your business to the next level, it's time to hire a Dream Team. *Hire Higher* is your guide to making smart, strategic hires that will help your business grow. Written by Andrea Hoffer, who has years of experience helping businesses find and hire the right people, this book provides step-by-step guides for hiring now and in the future. So, whether you're looking to expand your team or just want some tips on how to make smarter hires, *Hire Higher* has you covered.

—Allison Maslan, CEO, Pinnacle Global Network

Andrea Hoffer has taken her vast experience in the world of talent management and crafted a compelling yet concise book that frames a people-first approach. She inspires hiring managers to fully understand who they are looking to hire early in the process and customize the approach accordingly. *Hire Higher* provides compelling strategies and tools for continually upgrading the talent acquisition process in any organization. It also offers real-world insights on how to build winning teams for the long term with a useable framework. Attracting and acquiring top talent requires continuous action, effort, and focus and Hoffer makes a clear case for investing in a talent acquisition strategy, as it is a primary component to organizational success. This is an inspiring read for anyone that wants to build a team of top talent and will be a key resource in the toolkit for any hiring manager or talent acquisition professional.

—Traci Wilk, Chief People Officer, The Learning Experience

*Hire Higher* is a real-world practical road map to truly building your dream team. No fluff, just facts and solid advice from a real expert. Get this book before your competition does.

—Michael Altshuler, Speaker, Peak Performance & Sales Expert, Bestselling Author, Job Gladiator

Looking to hire the best people for your team? *Hire Higher* is your go-to guide. Andrea shares her proven steps and methods for finding top talent, so you can get the results you need. Whether you're a business owner or a talent professional, this book has what you need to grow your team successfully.

—Cesar Quintero, CEO, The Profit Recipe, Certified EOS Implementer, Speaker & Author

**HIRE HIGHER**

# HIRE HIGHER

## HOW TO ATTRACT, INTERVIEW & GROW YOUR DREAM TEAM

ANDREA HOFFER

**Hire Higher**

How to Attract, Interview & Grow Your Dream Team

Copyright © 2022 by Andrea Hoffer

Published by: Bexsi Publishing

All rights reserved.

No part of this book may be reproduced, stored in a retrieval system, or transmitted by any means, electronic, mechanical, photocopying, recording, or otherwise, without written permission from the author.

ISBN-13: 979-8-42838-429-1

# TABLE OF CONTENTS

Can behavior be predicted? .................................... 9

Chapter 1.  Discover WHO YOU Need. ........................ 15

Chapter 2.  How to Attract Your Ideal Candidates So They Are Knocking Down Your Door ...................... 35

Chapter 3.  How to Spot the BEST Candidates .................... 59

Chapter 4.  Making the Offer. ................................ 105

Chapter 5.  Onboarding ..................................... 121

Conclusion. .................................................. 131

Dream Team Membership portal ............................. 133

**INTRODUCTION**

# CAN BEHAVIOR BE PREDICTED?

When I was a child, there was a desk that sat in the hall outside my bedroom door. It was piled with research documents and letters, and I didn't really understand most of it at the time. The desk belonged to my great Aunt Bertha. While I never met her in person, I developed a deep bond with her because I was able to see myself in the life that she had lived. I felt a connection to her because I wanted to do what she did and push through the boundaries that life places in front of us.

In the 1930s, when most women weren't even considering going to college, my great Aunt Bertha earned a doctorate in child psychology. As I got older, I gained a better understanding of what she did in her work, and I started to recognize parallels between myself and her. When I read her doctoral thesis, I realized that she had spent much of her time analyzing children, trying to quantify their behavior and how it would affect them later in their lives. It was a process of conducting detailed assessments, determining values, and understanding motivation. Will this person be successful as an adult? Will they form lasting and valuable relationships? Will they be trustworthy? These were assessments about the fundamental characteristics of people and what this information would mean as they got older. Basically, could assessments predict behavior?

As I moved through my career, I realized that I was attempting to make the same type of assessments when it came to hiring employees. I was trying to figure out what kind of values the candidates possessed. Will they work cooperatively? Will they show up every day ready to solve problems? Will they be happy working here?

*People are wonderfully messy*

For whatever reason, I've always needed to fit people into categories. It's something my brain does instinctively. Over time, I've learned that people don't neatly fit into categories. We can come up with any number of different processes to try to achieve better results when hiring employees, but we can never account for the fact that people are wonderfully messy, and we can never fully understand a person without understanding everything about their lives. There will always be outside variables.

These variables led me to a desire to create a process that produces the kind of results that I need. It's not about reinventing the wheel so much as it's about making the necessary adjustments when parts of the process don't work as efficiently as they could.

The foundation of the process is understanding that everyone in an organization contributes something of value to the organization. The person who cleans up after everyone else has gone home has something just as uniquely important to contribute to the mission of the organization as the CEO. As people, we want to contribute value and grow as individuals. We want to see our efforts as important. We also want to be challenged, or we become bored and unhappy.

My mother worked for Bloomingdale's for many years, but she wasn't content to stay in the same position year after year. Instead, she made it her goal to keep pushing until she had made her way to the top. For her, that meant setting out on her own and starting a business once she had learned as much as she could from working for others. When she started out, she may not have had a specific goal in mind, but she knew that she wanted to face challenges and overcome them.

One of the most gratifying things that I hear from employees that I've worked with is that they appreciate me challenging them. I want to get people to the next level even if they don't know that is what they want yet. Of course, there's nothing wrong with being happy with where you are professionally if you're still growing and improving at what you do.

*Mistakes I have seen and made myself*

I've worked with business owners who were having trouble building their business at the rate they wanted. They were not seeing the growth they thought they would see. What I've found over the course of my career is that it is difficult to grow a business without the right team. It's having the right people in place to guarantee that your company performs the way it should.

Too often, I deal with business owners who feel like they can fill a position by posting it to a job board and just waiting for the perfect candidate to show up. Sure, you might get lucky, and the perfect person will magically wander into your office, but usually it takes more work than that. My goal with this book is to give you a resource that shows you where to start as well as a plan to get you to a place where you feel confident about the people you hire. We will spend time discussing the greater philosophy of hiring, but I also want you to have the tools to get started right away.

The first thing to keep in mind is that this is a long game rather than a short one. It is not an answer, but rather a road map. I'm not expecting that you will find a use for everything in this book. But I *do* hope that there are specific ideas that you can employ to improve your hiring practices and build a better team—a team that helps your business thrive.

My goal is to help you overcome the hurdles you are facing and create the right workforce instead of wasting money on job boards that alone, don't offer enough support and strategy.

You need to have a clear picture of who you need to hire. Not having a candidate persona is a mistake that I see quite often. I frequently observe companies who receive a giant stack of resumes from a job board. Is the right person somewhere in that stack? Maybe, maybe not. In some cases, it becomes clear that the hiring manager doesn't even have a concrete idea of who the "right person" is.

The second mistake is not having a hiring process. I once worked with a business owner who ran a spa business, and despite a passion for the business, she was only breaking even every month. She knew that she didn't have the right people working there, but she didn't know what to do about it, and as a result, she was spending her time putting out fires instead of focusing on the business itself. She had no process for hiring, and I knew that this was what kept her from success.

I spent some time coaching her, and we started to implement some processes that would allow her to refocus her attention on more pressing matters. This, however, was completely dependent on hiring good employees. After I had a better understanding of her day-to-day operations, we started hiring some new people, and we made sure that there was a process in place to train them for success in their roles. After a few months, my client came to me and thanked me because she had "fallen back in love with her business." When I work with clients, this is my ultimate goal. You started this company because you had a passion for it. But hiring the wrong people is the best way to destroy your passion. Suddenly, you're the one who must pick up all the slack because you don't have the right people in place.

This is something I didn't understand early in my career. I didn't know what separated a potentially good employee from a potentially bad fit. Once an employee is hired, you can see whether they are good at their job, but the goal of hiring is to identify the right employees *before* they start working with you.

Too many companies don't have a hiring process, and they don't have a hiring training program. Instead, they rely on resumes from the internet and a gut feeling about which candidates to hire. This is not a process. You might as well be picking names out of a hat.

Early in my career, I realized that I was making hiring mistakes, and at a certain point I realized there must be a better way to do this. Once I figured out what I was doing wrong, everything changed, and I wanted to start sharing what I had learned.

This book will go into depth about the hiring process and all the things you need to keep in mind as you evaluate potential employees. But the other part of the equation is retaining the employees you already have. While focusing on bringing in good new people is important, you also want to make sure your existing employees are happy. Are they still engaged with their work? Are they content with their situation or are they using their lunch break to browse the internet for a new opportunity?

One of the things I hear all the time is that turnover is too high. "Our business feels like a revolving door!" business owners will complain. Well, why do you think you're losing people? The answer may be that you are constantly short-staffed because you're not hiring good employees or that you are not setting your employees up for success or somewhere in between. Turnover just causes more turnover, and it's a cycle you need to break before you lose all your good employees.

I love to gain new knowledge, and I love to pass that knowledge along to others so they can benefit from it. Now that you've heard a bit about the common mistakes that you can stumble upon, I want to start talking about the steps you need to take to create your own hiring success. Being a business owner requires that you are resilient in the face of adversity. I learned these lessons the hard way, and my goal is to give you a guide that will help you avoid some of the challenges that I faced.

**CHAPTER 1**

# DISCOVER WHO YOU NEED

The first step to hiring the right person involves learning more about what you, as an employer, **bring to the table** and **what you expect** from your employees in return. If you don't do this work first, you are going to have a difficult time finding and recognizing the right hire. The six questions below will walk you through uncovering a clear picture of who a good fit for your position and culture would be. We will discuss each of these questions.

- Why does the position exist?
- What are the results/outcomes needed from this position?
- What skills and experience are needed to do this job successfully?
- What are the specific traits or attributes that make a person successful in this position?
- What are the specific behaviors that "fit" in our organizational culture?
- Why do team members stay with you, and why do they leave?

*Why does the position exist?*

Let's start with why this position was created. What is the overall purpose of this position? If we didn't have it, what wouldn't get accomplished? Don't list tasks here. What is the overall contribution that wouldn't get done if this position didn't exist? How does that contribution feed into the organizational mission? Look at the example below.

Example
**Job Title**:     Account Manager
**Job Purpose**:   To ensure clients' expectations are exceeded.
**Org. Mission**:  We help companies use internet marketing and sales technology to scale fast.

The Job Purpose for this position is, "To ensure clients' expectations are exceeded." It is that simple. The person who fills this position will know that everything they do will be with the purpose of ensuring clients' expectations are exceeded. This is measurable and there are many different responsibilities and tasks that can be done to accomplish this.

If we look at the Job Purpose along with the Organizational Mission, we can further define the value of this position and why it exists. The Mission is the reason the organization exists. It gives direction to the employees. The account manager knows that by elevating the client's experience, he or she is contributing to the mission of helping companies scale quickly by using internet marketing and sales technology. The Job Purpose is no longer in a bubble but understood as being part of the larger picture.

*What are the results/outcomes needed from this position?*

Now that we understand the overall purpose of the position, we must determine the outcomes needed from this position. This is where you define:

- Overall outcome (Outcome)
- How it will get done (By) – This is how they use their skills and experience to accomplish the desired outcome.
- How the results will be measured (Metric)

Example

**Job Title**:     Account Manager
**Outcome**:   Achieve monthly retention goal.
**By**:              Strengthen relationship with clients with weekly client updates and needs assessment.
**Metric**:       Retain 85% of client base.

You will notice that the outcome/result is observable and measurable. It is also specific – Retain 85% of client base. The responsibilities or tasks connect directly to the desired outcome. This is the format of a results-oriented job description.

Now ask yourself: What outcomes are you looking to produce with your position? On the surface, this doesn't sound complicated, but it can be a difficult question to answer if you go deeper than a simple job description. This is a place where things can become confusing.

A job description typically outlines the necessary skills, training and education needed by a potential employee. It will spell out duties and responsibilities of the job. This is the practical side of the equation, and it is important to be able to describe the position accurately and concisely. But, at the same time, you, as the hiring manager, need to be able to answer a different question before you can consider any of your candidates: What are the results you need from creating this position? If you are considering hiring a new team member for an existing position, or you are creating a new position, you need to understand what results this hire will produce that will be beneficial to the organization.

First, you will probably think about the tasks. What will this new employee be doing on a day-to-day basis? Again, this is the practical side of the situation. But before you can post a job, you need to understand how these tasks will contribute to the outcomes that you need. I call this a results-oriented job description. There are several different ways that we can assign value to a new hire, but one of the easiest is to put a dollar value on it. What is the specific financial benefit to the business for hiring this new employee?

Obviously, the goal of any new hire is that it pays for itself with improved productivity and then generates a profit. For most employers, a new hire equals more time to pursue new revenue streams. If the position is sales-oriented, it will be easier to see the financial benefits of new hires because you will be able to quantify their sales on a regular basis. If this allows you to shift your attention away from sales, you can see a clear benefit in the form of more free time for yourself.

Quantifying the contributions of other types of employees can be a bit more difficult. When we look at areas like operations and customer service, it's more difficult to put a dollar value on their contributions, but ideally, you will be able to develop a formula that tells you that these new positions will save you X many dollars per hour. Again, the goal of creating new positions is to give you the opportunity to spend your time growing your business rather than performing day-to-day tasks.

Because of this, you need to look at new hires as an investment in the long-term health of the business. I work with clients who worry about what new hires will cost them in the short term because they have trouble focusing on the long term. Yes, in the short term, new hires will cost more money because you must pay, train and provide resources for them. The problem is that if you never escape the trap of having to do too much day-to-day business, you won't have time to grow and you will stay stuck at the same level forever.

*What skills and experience are needed to do this job successfully?*

When I ask clients to list the skills and experience they want the person they hire to possess, they typically have little trouble coming up with a long list. The challenge becomes when I ask them to cut it down to 4 to 6 skills a candidate absolutely MUST HAVE to do the job. I ask them to consider the outcomes they need from the position. Which of the skills listed will help the new employee to accomplish those outcomes? Can any of those skills be taught and are you or someone on your team willing to take the time to train the new hire?

In the example below, our client was looking for an executive assistant (EA). She is a very busy CEO of a growing company. We knew she wouldn't have time to train someone on how to support a busy executive. She needed an EA who had done it before and was successful at it. She also needed someone who had basic skills with Office, CRMs and writing, since this position would have some marketing tasks. Each skill was considered in terms of the results our client needed from this position.

EXAMPLE
**Job Title:** Executive Assistant
**Skills:** Microsoft Office, CRM, Writing
**Experience:** Min. of 3-5 years supporting a busy executive or project

*What are the specific traits or attributes that make a person successful in this position?*

Success traits are the top qualities needed to be successful in a specific job. We need to have these traits in mind *before* crafting a job posting or conducting interviews. Unless an employee is successful in their position, you won't be able to step away from that aspect of the business. As a business owner, you want to craft an environment that is largely autonomous. You can't do this unless you can trust that all the moving parts are working correctly. The key to this is finding the employees with the right traits.

When I work with clients, I coach them to identify these success traits and then make those traits the centerpiece of their job posting and the main thrust of their interview process. Part of this is understanding that you can train a good employee to do their tasks, but you can't train an employee to have certain inherent traits that are necessary for success. Instead, you need to be able to identify candidates who possess these traits when they walk in the door.

It all comes down to who *you* are looking for. This is going to vary from business to business because the needs will change depending on the situation. But the more specific you can be about who you are looking for, the easier it will be to recognize that person when you see them.

Success traits come from looking at your best team members who have been in the position you are filling. Think of stories/examples of times these team members did something that you wanted to brag about. What traits or characteristics were they exhibiting? Below is an example taken from the EA position we were talking about earlier. Each trait is either measurable or easy to observe and presented as an action phrase. This is taken directly from the job posting we created for this position. It is written to not only attract the right candidates, but to encourage the people who don't relate to these traits to self-select out.

Don't skip this part of the process. Well-developed success traits become your answer key to the candidate interview. We will revisit this when you discuss interviewing.

EXAMPLE

**Job Title:** Executive Assistant

Prepare Ahead – You are always looking ahead to make sure you prepare the CEO for her next meeting, next day, and next week. You look deeper into things for missing details and then find them.

Collaborate – You recognize that while one of your roles is supporting our CEO, we are a team that works together. You are a strong collaborator and are ready to support the team as a whole.

Possess Confidence – You feel comfortable interacting with high-level executives and have the confidence to jump in and direct the CEO to her next meeting, if needed.

*What are the specific behaviors that "fit" in our organizational culture?*

Core values are the guiding principles that everyone in your company, no matter their position, live by and make decisions by each day. Your values drive your behavior. Essentially, your values are how you operate. These values are difficult to teach and are specific to your organization. The success traits describe how someone can be successful in their specific position. Core values are what everyone on your team throughout your organization lives by.

Identify four to six values that are most important to you. These values need to be consistently communicated and reinforced with your team. Too often, I see business owners who identify a list of values that are too broad, and my goal is to get them to narrow those values down to things that are more tangible in their daily life. How do these values "show up" every day?

I hear owners communicate values like "honesty" and "integrity" as their core values, but what does this really mean in a practical sense? How do these values show up? If it just comes down to your employees not stealing from the register, you need to think deeper than that. Employees following basic tenants of the law isn't really an individual value. It should be a given that your employees are honest. But this can often be a challenge for business owners because they haven't thought about their business in terms of a values-based philosophy.

When I start working with a new client, I always start with our Discovery Process. This includes a questionnaire and then our discovery session. We send our discovery questionnaire to several people at the company, not just the CEO. Interestingly, we often get a range of responses from these different people, but the themes tend to be very similar.

Once we've gathered the responses, we have a kickoff meeting to get everyone on the same page. The point is to clearly demonstrate what this company is about, and why that makes the company great. I draw stories out of the team members so that they can better articulate how they want the company to function.

The first thing I usually ask is for the team to think of the best team member they can remember. Sometimes, this person is still at the company, and sometimes they've already moved on. But I like to get the executives to think about a story that illustrates why you want that person to be a model for the rest of your employees. How can you get everyone to show up like that ideal employee every day? These are the values that determine the success of your business.

To illustrate this point, I'll share a story about one of the amazing team members at AHA! I work with a lot of wonderful recruiters and one who tends to see creative solutions to difficult problems. That is a concrete value that I try to promote. The ability to think creatively and be resourceful.

We're currently working with a company that owns souvenir shops in Big Bear Lake, California. If you've never been there, it's a beautiful resort community about two hours from Los Angeles. In the summer, it's packed with tourists for lake activities, and in the winter it's a popular place for skiing and snowboarding.

This company was considering the idea of opening another shop and a frozen yogurt place, but they ran into a problem: finding quality employees. This wasn't just a problem for them. It was an issue for all the employers in the area because Big Bear Lake doesn't have enough permanent housing. Most of the housing is for vacation rentals, and the town is far from an urban center.

Even if you have a good hiring system in place, a general lack of workers is always going to make hiring difficult. The recruiter working with this client took it upon herself to look for creative ways to solve this problem. What she found was a game changer for our client. She discovered there was a work and travel program that would bring people from different parts of the country, or different parts of the world, to your location for seasonal work; typically, these seasons last between three and six months.

She pitched this idea to the client, who thought that this might be a great way to hire enthusiastic workers for their high season. The recruiter even put together a plan for the client about how they could take advantage of the program. This wasn't really part of her job description. She had stepped outside of the box and found a way to offer something to the client that didn't involve our typical services but gave the desired result for the client. That kind of thinking is how I want my team members to show up for work every day. I want them to be enthusiastic about finding ways to solve problems.

We tend to think of "values" as vague concepts like "honesty" or "integrity," but as I mentioned earlier, these concepts don't apply specifically enough to a real business. Of course, you don't want your employees to steal or lie to your customers, but that's a low bar. Those values should be implicit. I'm more interested in the values that may seem less obvious, but which are more relevant to running your actual business. This is how I want my clients to think when they're coming up with a plan for their core values. What specific values will guide your decision-making every day?

Of course, this process is more than just coming up with a list of values. As leaders, we need to be the ones who model these values every day, and we also need to make sure that we are holding our employees accountable as well. Do our employees show up every day living these core values, or do they just pay us lip service? This is the difference between a team that truly works well and a team that will soon start to come apart at the seams.

How do we reinforce this? How do we stay mindful of these values daily? One of the strategies I implemented when I owned my spa was to connect the values to the every day—a reminder of how each individual team member "lived" one of our core values. Instead of a "good job" email, we came up with a postcard system. The card had our logo on one side and a list of our core values on the other. When I observed one of my team members really living one of the values, I'd give them a card with the specific value circled, and then I'd add a couple of sentences about what they had done, and why I was so impressed.

Having something tactile like a card rather than an email gave the employees a real sense of accomplishment, and it further reinforced their commitment to our core values. But then I realized something else: This didn't just have to come from me or the other managers. The employees could give these cards to each other when they witnessed one of their fellow workers do something that embodied our core values. Not only did this system reward employees for their actions, but it also allowed other employees to express their appreciation for each other. At first, I wasn't sure how well this would work, but then it took off.

At one point, I took a few days off, and when I returned to the spa, I walked into the office, and the walls were plastered with cards that employees had given each other. The break room walls were covered in cards too. I was absolutely overwhelmed by how enthusiastically the team had adopted the system, and it was obvious that it had not only improved morale, but it had instilled our core values even deeper into the team.

The part of the card system that really appealed to the team was the physical aspect and the fact that the cards could be tacked on the wall. It was all out in the open, and it was something that they could all take pride in. If you have a remote team, I suggest finding ways to make it easy to recognize team members in a public way. At AHA!, we use Slack and set up channels specifically for this.

Once this concept of the core values is properly ingrained in the culture of the company, you get to take advantage of one of its real benefits: You can delegate with the knowledge that your team members are accustomed to working based on these values every day. This produces another benefit: You don't need to babysit your team. If your team members show up the way you want them to show up every day, you are now free to pursue other things.

One of the keys to hiring successful team members is to not only understand your core values, but to use them as a guidepost as you recruit and evaluate candidates. We will discuss this further throughout this book.

*Why do team members stay with you and why do they leave?*

Every company is different, which means "a good fit" for one company isn't a good fit for another company. The discovery process is about figuring out what makes a candidate ideal for *your* business. This is the part of the process where you, as a business owner or hiring manager, need to get specific about what you want, but also what you offer. What kind of environment are you creating with your business? There isn't a right or wrong answer to these questions. It's just a matter of what you need and what you provide. A candidate who thrives in a quiet, laid-back atmosphere probably isn't going to thrive working in a fast-paced car dealership. It doesn't mean one environment is doing something "right" or "better," it simply means that different environments are going to be attractive to different people.

This also is a time to think seriously about the fact that employment is a two-way street. Both employers and employees can fall into a place where they see employment as being only a matter of *what can you do for me?* But if this is how you operate as an employer, you're not going to retain the best employees. And if this is how you operate as an employee, you most likely won't be retained as an employee because you aren't prioritizing the needs of the company. Instead, both sides need to operate with a fair give and take.

Therefore, the first thing you, as a business owner, need to consider is: What do I have to offer? Keep in mind that money isn't the only answer. Good candidates know that they're going to be paid according to their skill level, but what *you* have to offer are the things that other companies can't offer.

The things that you bring to the table are more about the culture you have created. What kind of atmosphere have you fostered? Do you encourage professional development? Good candidates will want to know this because good candidates are people who won't be satisfied doing the same thing for the rest of their lives. They will want to know that their hard work will pay off in ways that go beyond monetary compensation.

Remember, the goal is to avoid turnover. You need to be in a position where you're not firing bad employees, and you're also not losing good employees when they find better opportunities. Now, perhaps more than ever, you need to be aware of whether a position at your company is a *good* opportunity for your ideal employee.

At this point in time, there are plenty of good positions out there, and there are also plenty of qualified applicants. This means that the evaluation process needs to flow in both directions. A good candidate doesn't show up to an interview *solely* to be evaluated by a potential employer. A good candidate shows up to the interview ready to evaluate the employer as well.

Good candidates know that they are good candidates, and they expect to learn how and why this job is going to benefit their lives. And again, unless you plan to pay well above what other employers pay, you need to offer opportunities and benefits that aren't monetary. When I ask employees why they like working where they work, the answer is often as simple as: My employer is a good person to work for.

So, what does this mean? Good to work for. The word I hear over and over is appreciation. Too often, I encounter employers who think of appreciation and compensation as the same thing. Of course, your employees will appreciate their compensation, but they also expect their compensation. Appreciation is something that exists on a more human level. People value being appreciated because it validates them as a person. It makes them feel whole in a way that money cannot.

You might be wondering: How do I make sure that I show my employees that they are appreciated? I'm reminded of the story of the employee who performs his task perfectly and goes to his boss for kudos. His boss just shrugs and says, "You did your job. Do you want a medal or something?"

The problem is that too many employers see their employee's work merely as expectations. If expectations are met, there isn't any reason to show a higher degree of appreciation. But over time, employees start to feel as though their work is only relevant if they make a mistake. Then their boss reprimands them for the mistake, and this is supposed to serve as an incentive for better work in the future.

If this is your approach, your good employees will lose their will to exceed expectations because they never see any personal benefit from it. This isn't the kind of attitude you want to foster. You want your employees to give you their best, and the only way to do this is to give your employees *your* best.

One of the ways that employers can show their appreciation is to make the working environment more social. We've all heard the cliché that when you hear an employer say that "their team is like a family," it usually means that the hours will be so long that you will see your coworkers more than your actual family. But this doesn't have to be the case. The key is to find social activities that appeal to your team. Find out what they like to do, and schedule get-togethers that allow your employees to bond in a way that doesn't pertain to work. This is also a great way to spend time with your employees to find out how they feel about their position and whether there is some type of opportunity you could be offering them.

These activities are a great way to find out why your employees stay with you. Why do they like working with you? Why do they enjoy being a part of *this* company? Employers often feel as though their employees stay because this is the job they know how to do, and they need the paycheck. But the reality is that your employees could do the same job and receive the same pay at another company. You need to know why they've decided to stick with you.

The only way you can get this information is to really get to know your team. They need to be comfortable enough with you that they can share what they really think and feel about their job. And you also need to understand that their reasons will vary. Some employees might be drawn to flexible hours because it suits their lifestyle. Other employees might value the fact that they see a clear trajectory towards advancement. In some cases, employees value things that you hadn't even thought of until they tell you.

On some occasions when we're conducting our Discovery Exercises with clients, we'll ask other, current employees, to join us, and we ask them these questions directly. What do you love about working here?

At one point, we were working with a technology company. It was founded by a woman, and she owes part of her company's success to the fact that she clearly appreciates her team, and she goes the extra mile to be supportive of them. This level of appreciation became extremely meaningful to her team to the point where it became important that anyone who joined the team needed to recognize that level of appreciation. But at the same time, employees couldn't use that appreciation to take advantage of the company.

When I look at a company like that, I know that this component needs to be part of what we put out into the world when we're attracting new candidates. They need to understand what they will receive by taking this position, and they need to understand how important it is to the overall culture of the company.

The tech company I just mentioned didn't offer the biggest salaries in the tech field, but they did offer a competitive salary. If a candidate was simply interested in earning the highest salary, this probably wasn't the right fit for them. But what I found was that the candidates who *were* a good fit for this company valued things beyond the salary. They were attracted by the passion of the CEO and her vision for the company. It was a mission that they wanted to be a part of, and they valued the fact that their work was appreciated rather than taken for granted. For them, this was more important than a little more money.

We once worked with a mid-size healthcare organization. They were growing rapidly and functioned fast-paced and at times could even be considered disorganized. They knew that they lost team members who preferred a more organized, structured environment. We built on this when creating their job posting and recruitment marketing. The messaging centered around how this organization was looking for individuals who were entrepreneurial, enjoyed a fast-paced environment and thrived with little to no structure. Did this lower our application count? Absolutely! It also attracted more individuals who could be successful at this organization.

The goal is not to attract a large volume of applications, but to attract candidates who will be successful in your organization. Below are some reasons people stay or leave a job:

| STAY | LEAVE |
|---|---|
| • MISSION | • LONG HOURS |
| • LEADERSHIP | • TOO MUCH CHAOS |
| • TRADITIONAL BENEFITS | • PAY TOO LOW |
| • TEAM APPROACH | • MUST WORK WEEKENDS |
| • FLEXIBILITY | • NO ROOM TO GROW |
| • CELEBRATIONS | • TOO MUCH CHANGE |
| • COMMUNITY IMPACT | • LEADERSHIP |
| • APPRECIATION | • NO STRUCTURE |
| • GROWTH | • LACK OF TRAINING |
| • SECURITY | • DON'T RELATE TO MISSION |
| • ENJOYS THE POSITION | • TOO FAST-PACED |
| | • POSITION DOESN'T FIT WITH CAREER GOALS |

We've discussed that a vital part of a successful hiring process is attracting the right people. You can't hire the right people if you can't attract the right people. When we start working with a company that finds themselves in a position where they can't seem to bring in the right people, we start with the Discovery Exercises mentioned above. This is the foundation of what we do because without this process, we can't access the information we need to know who a good fit for the company is. Our Discovery Exercises build upon the six questions we discussed in the previous chapter. You can access our Discovery Worksheets on our Dream Team Membership portal at *http://www.joinaha.com/*.

Let's say you're in a position where you know what you are looking for in a candidate, and you know what you can offer a candidate. How do you get that candidate to walk through your door? How do you attract the talent that you need? In the next chapter, we'll go into depth about exactly how *you* can stand out to the candidates you want to hire.

**CHAPTER 2**

# HOW TO ATTRACT YOUR IDEAL CANDIDATES SO THEY ARE KNOCKING DOWN YOUR DOOR

*The job posting*

I'm a firm believer that the foundation of success in hiring is a great job posting. If you put the work in and develop a good job posting that clearly describes "who" will be most successful in this position and what you have to offer, you can use it as a guide as you screen resumes and interview. Additionally, your posting will draw the best-fit people in. A good posting helps candidates to start picturing their life working at your company. You want them to feel motivated to give their best when they come in for their interview because they can already see themselves becoming part of your culture. The job posting is also your best tool for developing your interview questions.

When you use your job posting as a roadmap for your interview questions, you will have the opportunity to craft questions that give you much more insight into whether or not this candidate is a good fit for your company and vice versa. This is why I coach my recruiters to always refer to the posting before conducting interviews. Every company is looking for someone different, even if they don't know it. In a superficial sense, every company is looking for responsible employees who will show up and do their very best every day. So, let's just assume that this is a given. On a deeper level, though, companies have different needs when it comes to the everyday.

Therefore, creating a well-developed job posting is so vital to your success. Unless *you* have a crystal-clear idea of who you are looking for, you won't recognize them when they walk into your office.

So, let's talk for a moment about the difference between a job posting and a job description. Too often, employers don't understand the difference between these two items, and as a result, they end up less prepared when they need to hire new employees.

A job description tells you about the job. It functions almost like a contract between the employer and the employee, and it mostly covers the outcomes that are expected and the tasks that will allow those outcomes to be met. It's a dry and business-like document, but it is important because it lays out the expectations for the job.

A job posting, on the other hand, is a piece of marketing. This is the document that attempts to sell the job to a qualified applicant. It identifies the core values of the company. It describes the type of culture that you can expect. And perhaps most importantly, the job posting talks about the traits you are looking for in an employee. Again, not just skills, but personal traits.

One mistake that I see often is employers and candidates relying solely on the job description. Employers end up casting too wide a net. They're not weeding out people up front because they're not telling potential candidates what they're looking for in a person. Instead, they're just describing a long list of daily tasks. They also aren't differentiating themselves as an employer.

In my experience, about 85% of candidates don't read the job posting all the way through. They review the first few sentences and either move on or send a resume. They're not concerned with learning whether they are a great fit, and instead, they look at the skills required in the description and figure they *might* be a good fit. Not surprisingly, many of these candidates end up at an interview only to realize that this job was never going to be a good fit for them. What kept the candidate from reading the job posting?

When it comes to crafting a great job posting, you need to think of it as a pitch. This is what is supposed to draw the candidate in and make them not only want to apply for the position but be invested in winning the position. The goal is to keep them reading so that they can absorb all the information that you need to communicate. This doesn't mean that they will read to the end of the posting and know for sure that they are a perfect fit for the company, but it will give them the information they need to decide whether they think it is worth their time to apply and interview. Your goal is to attract the kind of candidate you want while filtering out the candidates who just aren't the right fit.

When I start working on a new job posting, I like to start with a series of five or six questions that delve into the elements of this irresistible job. The goal of these questions is to make the potential candidate think about themselves and whether they can see themselves thriving in this environment. But at the same time, the questions are also designed to offer practical information about the job itself and the larger culture of the company. I want the candidates to think seriously about how they would fit into the world that I'm describing. If they read through it, and it sounds like a fantastic fit for them, great. But if they read it over and feel as though they're just not the right person, that's great too. I don't want to spend an hour interviewing a candidate who was never going to be a good fit.

What kinds of questions work well at the start of a posting? We tend to start off with something straightforward. If this is a sales position, we might lead with a question like: "Do you have experience working in sales?" It's a very basic start. Let's say the candidate has sales experience, so we'll move on to something a little more complicated like: "Do you want to be part of a team of advanced and innovative people that grow sustainable food?" We started with "Do you like to sell stuff?" And now we've moved on to: "Are you interested in selling *this* stuff? Is sustainable food something that has value to you? Is this something you believe in?" These kinds of questions are informative, but they're also designed to draw in the right candidate. The goal is to attract them to the job because the job appeals to them on a personal level. The other goal is for them to keep reading the job posting.

Keep in mind that when postings are published on job boards, you often only see the first few sentences when you are browsing. So, if you're going to draw people in and entice them to read the whole posting, those first few sentences need to capture their attention.

What too many hiring managers forget is that hiring is about marketing. You are selling your company and job opportunity to potential candidates. You need your candidates to understand your message. But too often, I see job postings that are just descriptions. There's no effort to woo the candidate with the opportunity you are offering.

Recruiting is marketing. There are, inevitably, plenty of qualified candidates out there. And these candidates can be hired by any number of companies. Your goal is to find the best of the best. But the best candidates know that they're the best candidates. They have the skills and experience, and they have certain expectations when it comes to their next opportunity. As a business owner, you want the best employee. But as an employee, you want the best job. For both sides of this to work, you need to make sure your company stands out as a great place to work.

Our goal is to marry recruiting and marketing so that we have a successful cycle of posting and hiring. This is where the discovery exercises come in. Through this series of exercises, you will gain a better understanding of your culture and the message you want to send to potential candidates. These exercises are designed to give you an insight into what you want and what you need, but also to allow you to understand how to articulate this in a way that is attractive and understandable to potential candidates.

All of this starts with language. The words you use in your posting can have an enormous impact on how the posting is perceived. Our system shows you how to use language to draw people in rather than turn them off.

This is something people rarely think about when they put together a job posting. How does the language you use affect the candidates who see it? We tend to see the world through our own lens, and this creates a problem because we can end up not seeing what others might see. Do certain words turn off certain people? This is important because you might lose high-quality candidates simply because of how you chose to phrase a single sentence in your posting. People from different backgrounds tend to react differently based on word choice, and what might not send up a red flag for you could be what makes a highly qualified candidate pass on your posting.

Part of what we do is analyze your posting to see if there is potentially problematic language that might be considered offensive or a turnoff for women or people of different cultural backgrounds. But it isn't always about being offensive, per se. Sometimes, it's more a matter of what different people find attractive when they read a job posting. Remember, a job posting is a piece of marketing, and it's how you start to sell yourself to potential candidates.

Because of decades of social conditioning, women and men tend to react differently to the way job postings are worded. Hiring managers often don't realize that the posting they put out into the world will be interpreted very differently depending on whether it is being read by a man or a woman.

Many studies have shown that when women approach a job listing, they tend to go through the whole thing to see if they truly possess all the skills and traits listed in the posting before applying. And these same studies have shown that men don't really care about that. They just apply and worry about those details later. If you are finding that your postings are attracting mostly male candidates, you may want to use the free tool listed below to evaluate the language in your posting: *http://gender-decoder.katmatfield.com/*

Let's break down the different elements of a good job posting to help you understand the best way to attract quality candidates for your position.

**Grab the attention of the right candidates with questions that focus on who a good fit would be.**

**Get them to say, "YES! That's me."**

Grabbing the candidate's attention with questions about them is a great way to start the posting. We suggest you use a few questions that really focus on the needs for the position. Here are some examples:

- ✓ Do you have construction sales experience? Are you self-motivated and an over-achiever? Do you easily develop industry relationships with key decision-makers? Do you have top-notch research skills and your own existing book of clientele?
- ✓ Do you enjoy working in a strong team environment? Does working in a fast-paced professional kitchen fuel you? Do you have experience working in upscale dining?

You may also want to include a question that speaks to what makes your culture great:

- ✓ Are you looking to be part of a family-owned business where every team member is passionate about helping our clients grow their business?

Transitional statement to keep them reading if they identify with the questions:

- ✓ Then we are looking for YOU!

**Tell them who you TRULY are and make it easy for them to learn more about you and your team.**

This is a good section to briefly mention your company's core values and provide links to website and social media. Keep this section only about who you are as a company and team.

**Let them know who you are looking for and how they can be successful.**

Keep this to 4 or 5 bullet points with short descriptions. A word or phrase followed by a short description works best here. Make sure to use, "you" statements. Example below.

- ✓ *Dependable* –You show up each day ready to be there for our customers and your coworkers.

**Share the skills needed to do this job.**

Briefly state 4 to 5 skills needed to perform the job.

**Describe the benefits and "What's in it for THEM."**

Be transparent. Outline the pay structure and range in addition to any other benefits you offer. Candidates want to know there is opportunity for growth and advancement. If you offer this, include it!

**Close with a "Call to Action." Include clear steps. Make it easy.**

- ✓ Include 2 to 3 screening questions that are built into the application form.
- ✓ Include a CTA statement like, "We are waiting to hear from you! Hit the apply button now!"

**Format posting to make it easy to scan.**

- ✓ Make easy to read sections.
- ✓ Add your company "personality" into the headings and body.
- ✓ If you are sharing the posting on a job board like Indeed, be sure to write out all links. If you make text linkable, it often does not show up as a link on the job boards.

As another bonus for you, take advantage of our Job Posting Wizard to create an Irresistible Job Posting: *http://www.joinaha.com/*.

Make sure you go through the Discovery Exercises we provided for you above first. The link to the worksheets on our Dream Team Membership portal will get you started.

*Putting money behind the message*

One of the questions I'm often asked is whether it's important to spend money to post job listings. Ideally, your process will be organic, and you won't have to spend money on postings, but there are times when it is in your best interest to spend some money to get more eyeballs on your listing.

The key is to make sure you're spending money strategically rather than haphazardly. I recently had a hiring manager come to me saying they were trying to hire for a truck driving position, and they spent $600 on Indeed for their posting. Much to their chagrin, they didn't get a single application. My first question was: "Why did you start with $600?"

The first thing to keep in mind is that there are a lot of job board options available, and Indeed shouldn't be your only option. Having your message in many different places is a great way to foster a more organic hiring process, but if you've decided that you want to pay for postings, don't jump in all at once.

Think of job posting as marketing. When a company starts to market a new product, they don't roll out their whole campaign globally. They test the market, and this is exactly what you need to do when you're trying to attract candidates. If your budget for job posting is $600, you don't want to spend all that money at once because you might be putting your entire budget around a message that doesn't work. The reality is that you won't know if you got your message right until it's out in the world.

When we work with people who want to experiment with paid posting, we start out slowly by spending a very small amount of money for a three-day campaign. This gives us an opportunity to test the waters and see what we get. The first thing I look for is the volume. How many applications are coming in throughout those three days? But at the same time, I'm also looking at the quality of the applications coming in. You may end up with a high volume, but very few high-quality applications. Conversely, you may end up with a low volume, but with a lot of high-quality applications.

If the volume is low, but the quality is high, we want to turn up the faucet and get more applications. This is when I recommend putting more money behind the posting to attract even more high-quality applications.

Sometimes, we find ourselves in a situation where both the volume and the quality of applications are low. In these cases, putting more money behind a posting on one site isn't the way to go. What this has demonstrated is that this source isn't attracting the right people. We need to branch out to more sources to attract more talent.

This process can be somewhat experimental because the conditions for hiring change based on geography and timing. As such, we need to tailor each campaign to fit that situation. Therefore, it's so important to cast a wide net. What worked last year might not work this year, and what worked in one part of the country won't necessarily work in another part of the country. This is also why testing the market is so important.

Before we sink a lot of money into a new posting, we want to make sure we're putting that money in the right places. We need to get a sense of the results for *this* individual campaign before we spend the whole budget. And as I said, these conditions change constantly. Right now, we're seeing a huge shift in certain industries because of the pandemic, and this has changed the face of hiring in numerous ways. A few years ago, the idea of offering signing bonuses for hospitality workers would have seemed insane. But now, employers are having a hard time attracting these workers. As a result, the way you market to these workers needs to change.

*Am I stuck with Indeed?*

Job boards like Indeed are great, right? You can post your ad to a well-known site and just wait for the applications to start rolling in. Well, maybe…. The problem with the big job boards like Indeed is that you might be casting too wide a net. Lots of applications are great but sorting through a mountain of low-quality applications isn't fun.

If you want to zero in on the candidates that are right for *your* business, you might find that you have better luck with niche job sites and social media. Hearing the words "social media" might have caused your heart to beat a little fast. Sites like Facebook or LinkedIn are huge, and it can be difficult to know where to start. But as big as Facebook or LinkedIn can be, the populations still tend to revolve around niche communities. People on LinkedIn tend to flock to other profiles that fall into similar industries as their own. Legal professionals tend to follow other legal professionals because it is more relevant to them. This gives you a great tool for outreach because you can refine your postings to places that apply to what *you* do.

Check out more job boards on the Dream Team Membership portal.

People have always been visual animals, but as technology opens more and more visual possibilities, we have become even more visually oriented. This means that a highly visual ad is going to get more attention than a text-only ad. Unfortunately, most job boards like Indeed limit your job postings to text only.

When our clients come to us, they usually have a text ad that they've been posting to job boards. What we do is take the content of that ad and transform it into a visual landing page that is sharable on social media and through email. You can easily post it to any social media platform, and you can encourage your existing team members to share it with their social media connections.

As I said a minute ago, people tend to gravitate towards people who work in the same field or share the same interests. If you have your team sharing your posting with people they know on social media, you are not just increasing your reach, you are targeting your message. But it can be even more personal than that.

I encourage business owners to go to their best people and get testimonials. Have them write just a few sentences about why they love working for your company. This is perhaps the most valuable content that you can put in an ad because people have become increasingly reliant on what their peers think. This explains the popularity of sites like Yelp and the multitude of different review sites on the internet. People want to hear from real people about their experience, not just some company-created copy.

This kind of message gives potential candidates insight into what working at your company is really like. But words need reinforcement. This is where the visual element comes in. People are drawn to content that has pictures and videos. Just adding one photo to a job listing increases traffic as well as the amount of time people spend looking at the listing. The goal is to bring your words to life and adding visual elements to your posting is the best way to do that. Instead of thinking of your posting as simply an informative document, think of it as an experience.

The goal is to give your candidates a better idea of what your company is about, and why they would want to work there. This type of presentation is typically called a landing page, and if you don't have experience building one, I would recommend having it done by a professional. But because there are so many people qualified to build landing pages, it shouldn't be too difficult to hire a real professional at a reasonable price. And yes, this will require a bit of an investment, but this truly *is* an investment in your business. If you want to attract the best talent, you need to create the best possible first impression.

The goal of this type of posting is to give prospective candidates the feeling of a day in the life of one of your employees. What can they realistically expect when they come to work for you? Too often, I see employers make the job posting all about what the candidate needs to bring to the table. Do you possess all these skills and personality traits? Remember, hiring is a two-way street. You, the employer, need to offer as much as you demand.

Therefore, it's so important to look to your team to help with recruiting. This doesn't mean they're out there knocking on doors and handing out applications. It just means that the people you trust are probably going to know other trustworthy people.

When I was running my spa, I had employees who wore uniforms. It lent the business a sense of credibility when you were at the spa, but it also created another opportunity. It was a sort of advertising that didn't really cost anything.

What I found was that one of my employees might be out shopping and they'd run into someone they knew. Their friend might see the uniform and ask what it was like working there. Because I had put in the time to hire and train great people, their experiences were positive, and they spoke highly of their positions. This led me to institute an incentive program where employees could refer a friend and receive a bonus if the friend was hired and stayed on for a minimum of three months.

You might notice that more and more companies are using this method of attracting both employees and customers. Credit card companies will give you bonuses if you refer a friend. They do this because they want more customers, but they use *this* method because they figure that qualified people know other qualified people. Because people tend to travel and socialize among people who are fundamentally like them.

As you can see, the hiring process is about outreach, but it's also about qualifying. In this chapter, we discussed how to attract candidates to your posting and ultimately to your hiring process. Using these techniques in concert with each other will boost your traffic, but once you've done that, you need to know how to spot the best candidates.

*Capitalize on social recruiting*

It is important that your company has a social media presence even if you don't personally engage in this way. Potential candidates will interact with you through your social media channels. They will follow your channels to learn about your culture and to get a true feel for what it is like to work at your organization. Some will even message you through these platforms. Be sure to have someone on your team responding to messages and posting comments.

Social media is a great place to highlight your team. Share stories about their accomplishment — on and off the job. Share their interests and why they love what they do. Encourage your team to become thought leaders and to share their expertise on your channels. Showcase the amazing people who work there. Then, encourage your team members to share the posts on their social media channels. This will widen your network to "friends" of your current team — another way to generate employee referrals.

Social media channels are also a great way to share your job opportunities for free. Facebook allows you to post jobs for free on your business page and accept applications. LinkedIn gives you both paid and free options. Even TikTok has entered the recruitment arena with TikTok video resumes. The feature is limited at the time of this book, but there are still many ways to use TikTok and the other social media platforms for recruitment. Below are a few tips to get you started.

- Find out what social media platforms your current team members spend their time on and the type of content they interact with. Build a presence on these platforms. Share content relevant to job seekers in general, like job search tips, and content specific to your industry.
- Use relevant hashtags to make it easier to find — #jobsearchtips, #digitalmarketingtips or #lifeatgoogle.
- Reach out to an influencer. Invite them to work a day at your company and post about their experience. You may even have an influencer or potential influencer already on your team.
- Learn how to optimize content on each of the platforms that your team members spend their time . Encourage your team to share your company content with their network as well as job openings when they come available.
- Join and engage in professional groups on social media. Share tips and resources. Most groups do not allow employers to openly recruit, but if they get to know

you and your company as a resource, they will think of you when looking for a new job. Encourage members to direct message you for free informational tips. Once they do, ask them if they would be interested in learning about working at your company.

The above tips will get you started using social recruiting to expand your network and promote your company as a great place to work. Keep checking the Dream Team Membership portal for up-to-date tips and information on social recruiting. It is an ever-changing arena.

*Sourcing passive candidates*

No recruitment book would be complete without a section on sourcing. To be successful at recruiting, you need to be very proactive and reach out to people you think could be a fit for your job. Of course, you must find them first. We call this sourcing. We use every resource we can find to connect with people with the right skill set and experience and reach out to them to essentially "sell" them the opportunity to be considered for the open job. This takes research, marketing and selling skills to do as well as time. Therefore, many employers rarely engage in "sourcing" and instead rely on candidates coming to them through job postings.

This section is designed to give you the basics of sourcing. We are generally looking for **passive candidates** when we source. These are potential job seekers who are not actively looking for a new position. They are typically employed and often open to learning about a new opportunity if it comes along. There are many ways to find the people to reach out to and methods to connect with them. We will review some of the most cost-effective and easy to do here.

- Connect with everyone you meet professionally and even not professionally on LinkedIn. Expand your network on LinkedIn to grow your potential pool of people to source from. The LinkedIn app on your phone makes it easy to connect with people when you meet them in person.
- Join groups on Facebook and LinkedIn. Post questions. Add insights. Become known. Encourage members to direct message you, then add them to your network. Search through the list of members and ask to connect with them.
- Make sure all your social profiles are up to date and clearly show what you do. Change your tagline on your profiles to "Hiring Great People to…" This way, people will know you are hiring when they check out your profile — which they will do if you are actively posting, commenting and sharing.
- Create your own groups for your talent pools. Constantly add value for the members. As your group grows, so does your passive candidate reach.
- Use the search functions on LinkedIn and other platforms to search for people with a specific skill set or even people working at your competitors.

Get your list together of potential people to contact and reach out to them! Below will get you started.

Once you have identified people who may be a fit for your opening, you want to reach out to each of them individually. DO NOT SEND A BULK message. If you do want to send a message to several people at once, make sure you are using a platform that allows you to customize each message, so it looks like they were the only one receiving it.

We provided a couple of messaging templates for you to use on our Dream Team portal. If you know someone personally, you can add a bit of a personal message. Otherwise, keep it short and direct. Make sure you introduce who you are and why you are contacting them early in the message. Then ask them if they would like to learn more. Sometimes they will be willing to schedule a call with you right away. Often, they want you to send them information about the company, position and compensation before they commit to anything further.

There are many ways you can connect with potential candidates. We are going to concentrate here on a few of them.

## LINKEDIN

This is one of the best methods to reach out to potential candidates. Make sure your personal profile is up to date and that it shows the company you work for or own. Potential candidates will check out your profile first before replying to your message. They want to see that you and your company are legitimate.

Depending on your membership with LinkedIn, you have different options to contact people. If you have a free membership or Premium with limited messaging, you will want to message by sending a connection request.

1. Find the person's LinkedIn profile.

2. Click the More button and it will give you a dropdown box. Click Connect.

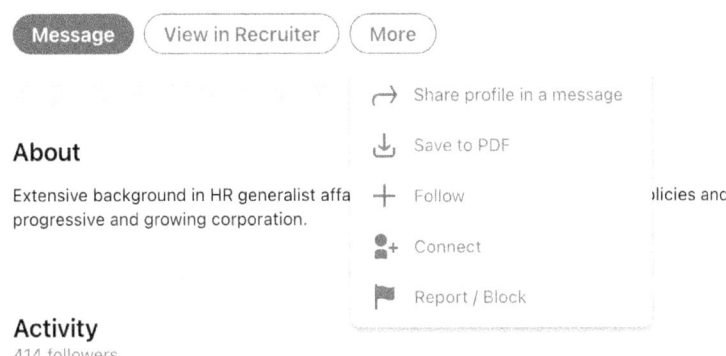

3. The following box may appear depending upon the person's settings. Click Connect.

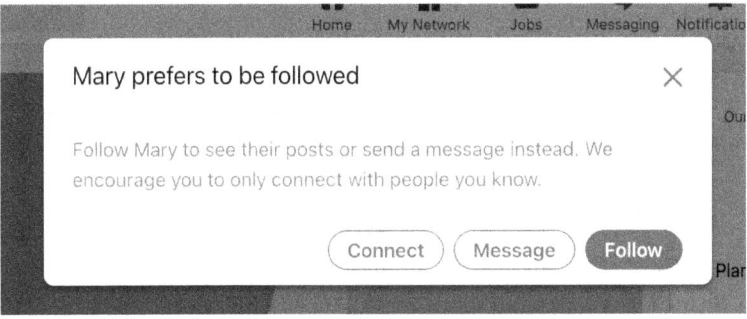

4. Your connection request has been sent, but now you need to add a note. Click Add a note.

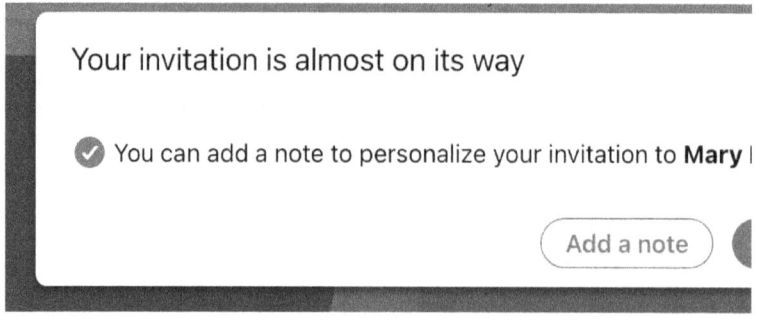

5. This is where you use one of the messaging templates we provided for you in the Dream Team portal. It is also a good practice to add the following to the message:

"I'd still love to connect here even if you are not interested in our job opening."

This will help you build your LinkedIn network for the future. If they connect with you and/or write back saying they are not interested in leaving their current position, always reply with: "Thank you for your response. If you know anyone who may be interested and is a good fit, I'd appreciate it if you could connect them with me."

This often pays off.

## EMAIL

The messaging is similar with email, but you will need to get their attention right away and show you are not SPAM.

*Use the subject line*

Here is a good subject line you could use: "(COMPANY) is HIRING a (POSITION TITLE)"

Gets to the point.

One thing you can do with email that you cannot do on LinkedIn is send multiple messages. We recommend sending a total of three emails and spacing them a couple of days apart.

This also allows you to test out different subjects and messaging.

## TEXT

Some argue text has replaced calling potential candidates and others still say a call is best. We have found we get a better response with texting. It is low investment in time for people. We all are weary of picking up a call from someone we don't know. Texting allows you to introduce yourself and your reason for contacting them without the receiver having to answer a call. Plus, a large portion of the workforce is part of a generation that prefers texting to calls.

Messaging is the same with texting. Introduce yourself, the company and the position opening. Ask if they want to learn more.

**Don't use just one method**

Everyone has multiple communication methods. We suggest you use at least three for each person you reach out to. You can mention in email or text that you also messaged them through LinkedIn. This way, they may log into their account and learn more about you before deciding to respond.

In chapter two, we talked about how to get your message out there and how to be noticed once you put your posting into the world. Because the reality is, if no one knows you exist, you won't get any bites from prospective candidates. But now that the floodgates have opened, and you have an avalanche of applications coming in, how do you identify your ideal candidate? Chances are, you're going to receive more than one application from qualified applicants, but how do you narrow the qualified people down to the ideal people? This can be a challenge, but it doesn't have to be if you know who you are as an employer, and you know who you're seeking.

Earlier, I said that one of my early hiring mistakes was to just hire whoever walked in when I needed to fill a position. I wasn't asking myself, *is this the best candidate for the job?* I was just thinking that this person might work out, and if they did, my life would be a lot easier. The problem was that I wasn't asking, *what if this person doesn't work out?* Along the way, I started to understand what makes the best candidates stand out from the rest. In chapter three we're going to go into depth about how to spot these candidates and how to guide them from ideal candidate to star employee.

**CHAPTER 3**

# HOW TO SPOT THE BEST CANDIDATES

*Why you need a hiring process*

In my late thirties, I invested in a spa franchise concept. It was my first business. I sold my condo and moved back in with my parents to make the business a reality. It was a challenge, but all the pieces were coming together except one. I was running into a particular problem with the people I hired to work at the front desk. If you've ever been to a spa, you know that the front desk is a very demanding position. Instead of having a detailed hiring process in place, I was hiring people who just walked in the door and filled out an application. Typically, I would have a brief interview with them, and that was it. If I liked them, I would hire them on the spot. Sound familiar?

It shouldn't have come as a surprise that it became a revolving door of front desk employees. I started to realize that this wasn't just creating more work for me, it was tarnishing the image of the business. The person at the front desk is the first person that the customer interacts with. This is the face of the business, but I wasn't putting in the work to hire the right people for the job. This meant that I was always at the front desk helping clients instead of working on growing the business.

At a certain point, I had had enough, and I knew that I needed to make a change. I knew I needed to step back and create a process that I could use for hiring or I wasn't going to be able to keep the business afloat much longer. I pulled on processes I had learned and been a part of in my former positions as well as best practices that I found being used today to create a process I thought could work for my needs.

What I also realized was that the process I was developing could be used by other professionals who were also frustrated about their hiring difficulties. It was a targeted process for hiring frontline employees, specifically. At the time, I didn't realize that this would evolve into a recruiting business because I was focused on solving the problem in front of me. Later, I realized that I wasn't the only one struggling with this.

As you may have guessed, a lot of business owners don't have a concrete hiring process. They often "follow their guts" when it comes to making decisions, and this is usually a less than efficient way of doing things.

First, you need to make sure you're looking in the right direction. Are you prioritizing the candidates who will improve your company and help you move forward? Do you know what kind of traits and skills will help you thrive?

What I tend to hear over and over from business owners is that they hire people that they "just fall in love with" right away.

This usually means that a charming person who reminds the owner of themselves comes in and works their magic. This might be the right hire if you need someone to work a sales floor and create lightning-fast rapport with your customers, but that doesn't mean this person is going to fit your culture.

Often, when I talk to business owners about their hiring process, I find out that they don't have one. This is a red flag, but it's also a good place to start. I once worked with a client I'll call Brenda, who didn't know what she was doing wrong.

"I just don't know. I think I just fall in love with everyone during the interview," Brenda said with a frustrated look on her face.

"And then what happens?" I asked, already half sure that I knew the answer.

"Well, they just end up taking advantage of my good nature," she said holding back tears. I could tell that she'd been through this before, and it felt like talking to someone about a bad dating history. She was worried that her instincts were off, and she didn't have the confidence to take another chance.

"I just don't know what I'm doing wrong," she said looking out the window.

A day or so after I spoke with Brenda, she called me and told me that she decided that she loved a person she interviewed. She wanted to make an offer immediately. She also shared the interview transcript with me.

"I'm going to play devil's advocate with you, if that's ok," I said, leaning in a bit. She nodded yes.

"Ok, Brenda, it's great that you love her. She does seem like a great person, but as far as her interest in the position you need done..." and then there was a moment of silence.

"What about her interest?" Brenda asked.

"Well, it's just that there were a few things that she said that made me think that she might not be a good fit for *your position*." I could tell Brenda was taken aback by this. Once again, she had unwittingly followed her gut, and I was contradicting her instincts. "When you asked her about what she enjoyed doing and what she didn't enjoy doing, it gave me a sense that she might not actually enjoy doing this job in the long term," I said as gently as possible.

"I don't know, Andrea. She did the team interview, and she just got along great with everyone," Brenda said.

"I get that. I do, but sometimes a person is a perfect fit for your culture, but they're not such a great fit for the actual position. Do you know what I mean?"

Brenda thought about it for a moment. I hoped that she was absorbing what I was saying because it really is true. You can find a candidate who has a stellar personality, and they're also a genuinely good person who works well with others. Those are all great qualities... unless that person doesn't enjoy the actual tasks they will have to perform.

"So, you think she might come on board and get burned out doing the job?" Brenda asked.

"I think that might be what's happening here," I said. "Let's keep going. We have other people to send you, and I think we can find someone who is the right fit for your culture as well as the position."

"Ok, let's give it a shot," Brenda said hopefully. "I just don't want to keep repeating the same mistakes, and it feels like that's what I was about to do."

By the time we got to the third candidate, Brenda started to see the difference that I was talking about. She liked this candidate as well, but she started to see the nuance between a candidate who would be a good fit for her and the culture of the company, and a candidate who could check those boxes in addition to being a good fit for the *position*.

It's common for us to talk people out of hiring someone. It's not because they're bad people, but because we want to make sure the person fits the company in several different ways. Some employers are charmed by personalities, but that doesn't mean the candidate has the requisite skills. Sometimes employers are too focused on skills, and they don't look for other factors like motivation or how this person will fit with the culture of the company. Our goal is to get employers to look at the whole picture because all these things will be important once the new employee is trained and working.

*Make It Easy*

For a moment, though, let's back up to the application process because this is an area that has been getting more complicated, and I think a lot of employers are going in the wrong direction. As an employer, you must understand that when you put a job posting out into the world, it will be seen by a lot of prospective candidates. And these candidates will often be looking at the posting on their phone.

What I have been noticing more and more in recent years is employers making it too difficult to apply for their job. They make the candidates jump through all kinds of hoops before that person even knows very much about the company. In some cases, I see postings that require extensive effort just to apply.

My guess is that these employers feel that they will narrow down their applicant pool if they make their application process extensive, but what they don't consider is all of the top-notch talent they are missing because they've made their application process too time consuming or complicated.

Instead, I counsel employers to make the application as easy as possible. Provide an easy apply button on your posting so all the candidates must do is upload their resumé. Job boards like Indeed and LinkedIn make this easy to set up. Once you have their resumé, you can decide if this candidate is someone you want to pursue. At that point, you can ask them for more information.

When I first opened my spa, allowing candidates to apply online instead of requiring them to complete a paper application was a big deal. Today, we create branded QR codes that point right to the online application for our clients to display in their place of business or hand out as business cards. The applications are short and typically can be completed with a few short clicks. Most people will apply with their cellphone, so you want to capture their information at that moment and not make it difficult to complete.

So, let's take a minute and review the key points of the process. As we go through this, keep in mind that the most important piece of the puzzle is making the process easy instead of difficult. I've watched plenty of good talent pass on applying for a job simply because the application process was needlessly long and complicated.

– Make the process easy instead of needlessly difficult.

Too often, I see employers feel as though prospective candidates need to prove themselves before they even have an interview, but we must keep in mind that everyone's time is valuable. If you set up a hiring process that requires a significant amount of time, and there isn't any guaranteed payoff for the applicant, they can decide that the process is a waste of their time. Respecting the value of everyone's time demonstrates that you have respect for your candidates even before you meet them.

– Put all the candidates go through the same process.

This is as much about fairness to the candidates as it is about creating a consistent process for you to follow. If you want to know, objectively, how your candidates perform as they travel through the process, there needs to be an objective process for them to follow. Lacking this step can be the result of carelessness because you haven't bothered to create a concrete set of steps to follow and questions to ask, or it could be a matter of "going with your gut." I've had employers tell me that they want to hire someone because they've worked with this person before. Because of this, they don't feel as though it's necessary to put them through the same process they might use with someone they don't know. While you might trust the person you know, *you* don't know if this person is the right fit for *this* position. Unless you put them through the same process as everyone else, you can't accurately tell if they're the best candidate.

The other reason putting everyone through the same process is a matter of the law is if you use one set of questions for one candidate and another set of questions for another candidate, it can be perceived as bias.

– Don't skip steps.

This one is tricky because it can be tempting to start abbreviating your system once you feel comfortable with it. Keep in mind that every step in your process is there for a reason. Each step allows you to learn necessary information about the candidate, and each step allows the candidate to learn about the position. Remember, you don't want to hire employees who realize too late that they don't want to do this job. This is just a waste of everyone's time.

– Communicate.

We have an interested candidate, what next? Once the candidate has applied, you reach out to tell them that you will follow up with them to touch base within three days. This keeps your candidates in the process. Many applicants feel as though they are just sending their information out into a void. Will anyone even look at it? How long should they expect to wait before getting an initial response?

I've heard from prospective candidates that they often send resumes only to wait months before hearing back from anyone about their application. If you want to attract the best talent, you can't keep them waiting. The best people will find something else.

Too many employers just don't understand the role communication plays in hiring the best people. You need to make yourself available to your candidates long before the interview process begins. You need to be able to answer questions they might have about the position. I've seen plenty of situations where a candidate went through the entire hiring process only to find out late in the game that this wasn't even a job they wanted. This is a waste of their time, but it's also a waste of *your* time. When it comes down to it, you want to do as much as you can to narrow down your field of candidates, so you are only interviewing the right ones.

Don't let the applications pile up. While it might feel nice to have a giant file of people to choose from, the best applications in there aren't going to wait around for you to catch up. You need to stay on top of applications as they come in and act on them immediately. A slow response indicates something about your business. At the beginning of the application process, your candidates approach your business in much the same way your customers do. They don't know a lot about you yet, but they want to find out if they want to do business with you. A slow response to an application tells the candidate that this is the kind of treatment they can expect from you if hired. A good candidate doesn't want to work for a company that doesn't treat their employees well.

Another tip to keep in mind is you want to make sure that you are reaching the applicant. What I've found is that email is becoming a slow means of communication for a lot of people.

Because of this, we respond via email, text and sometimes even LinkedIn InMail. Many applicants are more likely to communicate through text rather than email. You also need to consider that your emails might end up in junk folders while a text message usually gets immediate attention.

The other reason I find text messages helpful is because it feels as though a real person is reaching out, while email can often feel impersonal and automated. We also tend to reach out several times just to make sure our message is being received.

I've had colleagues say that if you send a message and you don't hear back, just move on. I disagree. I think it should be the other way around. To me, the applicant should be the one who moves on if they don't hear back from you quickly. A slow response is a clear message to an applicant that they aren't a priority. That is a red flag for applicants. Ideally, you don't want applications to sit around because you will lose good people in the shuffle.

The other thing to keep in mind is that you won't get a full picture of a candidate from their resumé alone. You may have questions that need to be answered before moving on to the next step. The goal of opening communication early on is to make sure the communication flows both ways. The employer should feel as though they are getting a clear picture of the applicant, and the applicant should have a clear picture of the company and the position.

*Screening resumes*

The first thing that I look at when screening a resume is tenure. How long has the candidate been at their current or last position? How about their last three positions? Did they jump from job to job every six to twelve months? Did these jobs have anything to do with the job I am offering? Had this person learned skills at any of these jobs that would be relevant to my open position? Another thing to keep in mind is if your opportunity fits with the candidate's career path. Sometimes this is difficult to tell from just a resume. That is one of the reasons we use one-way video interviews as our next step in the process.

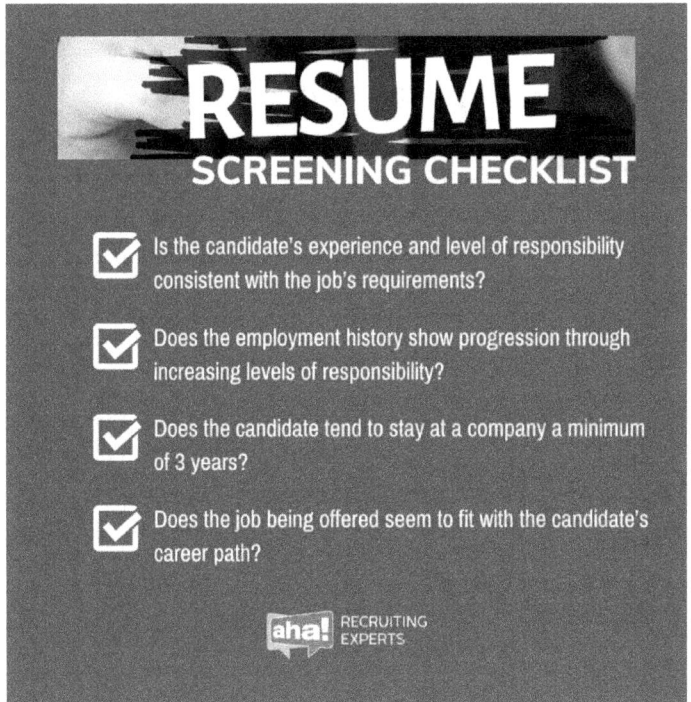

*One-way video interviews*

When we consider applicants, the first thing we ask them to do is make a short

video. This works as a one-way interview in which the candidate can introduce themselves. This doesn't have to be anything complicated.

The key is to make this process as easy as possible. Just because a candidate doesn't have advanced video making skills, doesn't mean they aren't right for the job. Unless, of course, the job involves making videos. We use our proprietary software, AHA! Hire, that is specifically designed to do one-way interviews as well as organize other parts of the hiring process. This way, they don't have to figure anything out to complete the process, and they can do everything from their phone.

Ideally, I want the applicant and the employer to feel as though there is a level playing field—that both parties are informed about who they are and what they do. I've seen plenty of job postings where there is no indication of who the company is or what, specifically, the job will entail. They list a bunch of vague requirements and duties, but for some reason, the details of the job are kept secret. I honestly can't imagine any good employee looking at that and wanting to apply. As an employer, you need to sell yourself to potential candidates just as much as they need to sell themselves to you. You both need something, and you both have something to offer. It's best to just be honest about this up front.

We highly recommend including one-way video interviews in your process because it can give you a better sense of the person behind the resumé before you invite them for a more formal interview. But again, this needs to be a two-way street. We encourage our clients to offer a video to their applicants as well so the applicant can get a better sense of the company before they commit to a long hiring process. Again, the more information both parties have, the better. This will help you weed out candidates that don't seem like a good fit, and it will help your candidates decide if you are a good fit for them.

Typically, the person in the company video will either be the hiring manager or the CEO, and this video shouldn't be very long at all — no longer than a minute. The main content of the video should be a show of appreciation to the candidate for applying and showing interest in the company. Then you can move on to who would be a good fit for the job. This will inform the candidate about what you are looking for, and this can be very helpful in terms of what comes next.

If the candidate looks at the video and realizes this is exactly the kind of place they would like to work, great. But if not, you have just saved both yourself and the candidate some valuable time. The other thing I like the CEO to include in the video is a bit about how making one-way videos can feel a little uncomfortable. After all, you're putting yourself out there in an unusual situation, and you don't get any direct feedback. Because of this, I like for the CEO to acknowledge this and relate their own discomfort with making their own video.

What this communicates to the candidate is that it's ok to be nervous when making their video. They're not being judged based on whether it's an Academy Award-winning performance. Most of all, we want them to relax and show us a bit about who they are.

I've found that video opens a world of possibilities because people tend to respond more favorably when they have something to look at. It adds credibility to your organization, and it allows the applicant to feel as though they know more about what they're potentially getting themselves into.

Generally, when a client attaches a video to their job posting, the response rate is far higher. We've also found that when the client offers a video first, the applicants are more likely to volunteer their own videos. But ultimately, this is all about putting a face on something that can often feel very impersonal.

You can also consider using video before you get to this step in the process. We're used to seeing text-only job listings, or maybe there's a photo included, but why not add a video when you are announcing an available position? This allows you to sell the job more effectively to prospective applicants because the job will appear more human.

Now you've cast your net. What now? The next part is screening. Hopefully, once you've posted your listing, you get a lot of interest. Once you've looked through the resumés and watched the videos, you can narrow down your pool to the candidates who you feel are the best fit. But the next step is to narrow it down further. You're busy, and you don't want to interview fifty different people for each position. Therefore, conducting effective phone screens is important.

*The phone screen*

We always start the interview screening process over the phone. I know, your natural inclination, especially now, is to set up a Zoom call. This part can come later. I've found that it's very helpful to see how an applicant shows up on the phone, especially if the position requires them to spend a great deal of time on the phone.

People can create a very different impression over the phone rather than on Zoom. This way, you can get a sense of their manner and how they carry themselves when they can only use their voice.

There are three goals to conducting a phone screen:

Format:

1. Determine if the candidate has the experience and skills to do the job.
2. Gauge how interested the candidate is in YOUR position.
3. Begin to see if the candidate is a good fit for your organizational culture.

- One to two questions around career/job fit. How does this position fit into their career plan? Do the future growth opportunities you see for this position match their career goals?
- Three to four questions around skill fit. Use the question format we discussed in the Crafting Interview Questions section below. Get SPECIFIC details of what they accomplished in the past.
- Three to four questions around cultural fit. Each question should relate back to one or more of your organizational core values.

- What questions do you have for me? Write down what they ask. This will remind you of what is important to the candidate.

Phone interviews usually last around twenty-five to thirty minutes using this format. Make sure to leave time at the end of the call for the candidate to ask questions. As a hiring manager, you always want to encourage your candidates to ask questions. This will help them understand exactly what they're getting into, and it will give you a better chance to get to know them and their concerns about the job.

One of the points that I feel needs to be repeated because I see so many businesses overlook it, is sharing the results you expect to see from the person who takes on the job. What results do you need to see for this person to receive an excellent performance review in 90 days?

As I mentioned earlier, I used to own a spa that had one very glaring problem: the turnover at the front desk was constant. Sometimes, it felt like I was turning over front desk employees daily, and at first, I didn't understand why. The applicants appeared to be qualified, but then they'd just quit.

What I started to realize was that I wasn't educating my applicants about what the job was all about. They went into the application process with an idea of what the job would entail, but then reality didn't match up with their expectations. And I realized it was my fault because it was my job to educate them *before* I hired them.

It became clear to me that the impression people have about working at a spa was that it was a laid back, relaxing place to work. The position I was offering was a high-volume sales position that also involved constant customer service. The customers at a spa are the ones who are there to relax, not the employees.

I found myself conducting one-on-one interviews where I would try to go over the main points of the job and the fact that it was customer service oriented. And the applicants would tell me that, *oh, yes, I can do that. No problem.* But the real problem was that they still didn't have a good enough understanding of the actual job or if it was the right fit for them. For some reason, the one-on-one interview just wasn't communicating what I needed them to know, and their responses to my questions weren't telling me if they were up to the challenge. I realized I needed a new system because the revolving door was hurting my business. That is when the group interview became part of my process.

*The group interview*

One of the things that I felt was missing from the traditional interview process was that it was too far removed from the job itself. You can ask a person a series of questions about themselves and their experience, and they will answer as well as they can, but as a business owner, I didn't get a real sense of this person, and this person didn't get a real sense of the job they would be doing. They might say what I wanted to hear, but that didn't mean they would perform well in the real world. That led me to consider how I could refine the interview process in a way that would be more informative for me *and* the candidate.

We often assume that everyone who applies for a job desperately wants that job. And we also assume that this will mean that they will perform the job well no matter the responsibilities. What I eventually learned was that this is a trap. Sure, a person who applies for a job wants a job, but that doesn't mean they want *this* job. The problem is that many businesses don't properly educate their candidates about what the job will entail. This may not seem important when you're hiring hourly workers, but when those workers become overwhelmed, or they're simply not suited to the work, you end up with that revolving door problem. This is what happened to me when I owned my spa.

Different people want different things out of a job, and this doesn't have anything to do with their quality as a worker. Some people love interacting with customers and selling. Other people prefer to work in a less customer-facing role where they can work independently. The person who loves interacting with customers isn't necessarily a better employee, they just thrive in a different environment. If you drop the person who prefers to work behind the scenes into a customer-facing role, they aren't likely to thrive, and they will probably leave their job.

The concept of the group interview allowed me to get a better understanding of who these applicants were, and whether they were suited to the role we were offering. In some cases, applicants learned more about the job during this process, and they became excited about moving on to the next step. But we also had applicants who said, "You know, I learned a lot here, but I don't think this is for me."

That might sound like a rejection, but I loved hearing this because it meant that the process was working. We were weeding out the people who didn't fit that role, and the people who moved on knew enough about the role to know that they wanted to do it.

Developing this process was an experiment, but once I started to see the results, I realized that I had figured out something significant. I also realized that this could be applied to other businesses and roles.

When we started doing this, we'd invite six to nine people at a time, and we'd host the interview at a local coffee shop. This way, they weren't interviewing onsite. It was a neutral territory. And instead of basing the interview around a question-and-answer format, we made it exercise based. We wanted to see how the candidates carried themselves while dealing primarily with each other.

The idea of this system was to give us a better idea of the applicants because we would be able to evaluate them in a different setting, but it also allowed us to see how they interacted with each other. This turned out the be the most important aspect of the system because we started to see how they worked in a team.

As I said, a lot of our applicants were people who liked the idea of working in a spa. They pictured the job completely wrong, and my mistake was not educating them properly from the outset. You might think that the most important qualities for employees at a front desk are being friendly and organized, but a spa is basically just a store that sells experiences. Our goal was to sell as many of those experiences as possible. The problem was that I wasn't hiring people who loved to sell. I was hiring perfectly friendly people who ended up feeling overwhelmed by the fact that they weren't posting the kind of sales numbers we needed to stay in business.

The group interviews gave us an insight into our applicants' behavioral motivation. Were they the kind of people who showed up to work every day motivated to sell? Or were they just pleasant people who had a good phone manner? Some people find the idea of selling to be uncomfortable and frightening. That doesn't mean these people aren't warm and welcoming people. It just means that they're not a good fit for a role that involves selling. When we used a less in-depth hiring process, we ended up hiring very nice people who were friendly with our clients, but they didn't excel when it came to pitching additional products. Our hiring process wasn't giving us enough information about our candidates. But once we modified the system, we started hiring candidates who were enthusiastic about *all* the duties we needed them to perform.

People who love to sell see selling not only as a challenge but helping someone who needs what you are offering. Making the sale is an accomplishment. It means something to them, and if you operate a business that requires closing sales, these are the people you need. This is very different than customer service. Just because you can offer hospitality, doesn't mean you can (or want to) close a sale.

What I didn't realize when I opened my spa was how important this distinction would be. Like many of my clients, I would tend to hire people quickly based on how much I liked them. Then would come the realization that they felt uncomfortable trying to sell a product to a customer.

The reactions I got from the group interviews were also very instructive. Some people would come up to me at the end, their eyes beaming. They had a great time, and they couldn't wait to move on to the next step. While others would tell me that it was an interesting experience, but it just wasn't right for them. Once I started to see these reactions, I realized that I was finally getting the information I needed, and the applicants were getting the information they needed. The system worked.

I didn't expect my front desk team to stay in their jobs forever. Inevitably, it would be time for them to move on to another opportunity or further their education. But now we had a talent funnel in place. It didn't feel like we were going back to the drawing board every time we lost a team member.

If someone was headed off to college in a couple of months, I didn't have to worry that we wouldn't be able to find a good replacement. One of the mistakes I see a lot of businesses make is only interviewing when you have an open position. But if you have an open position, or you know that a position will open soon, you are at the mercy of whoever applies *right now*. If you are regularly interviewing new candidates, you have a pool of talent to choose from at any time.

We kept holding the group interviews on a quarterly basis to keep that funnel full of talent. And if we came across a candidate who jumped out to us as an obvious superstar, we might hire that person even if we didn't have an open position.

It was right around this time that the business finally became profitable. Putting a greater focus on finding people who wanted to do this particular job rather than just hiring whoever walked in the door had an obvious and profound impact on our bottom line. And because our new employees were already sales-minded people, we could coach them further. I've worked with businesses where the owner brings in sales training, and it doesn't lead to an increase in sales. These owners are usually frustrated because they've invested a significant amount of money in training, but they didn't see results. The hard truth is that if you don't have the right people, training won't help. As I said before, some people naturally gravitate towards selling. These are the people who you can train to become expert sellers because they want to learn.

Your best employees are the ones who want to show up each day because they like what they do, and they feel as though their work is being appreciated. This is very different from simply wanting to have a job. Wanting to have a job fulfills a basic need for personal security, but if the employee isn't a good fit, that need for security is overtaken by the desire to move on to a different opportunity. Our goal was to improve retention, and this is how we accomplished it.

*Phone role-play*

I realized that a big part of the front desk position was speaking to clients on the phone. So, why not make a phone interview part of the process as well? I mentioned earlier how people tend to behave and respond differently depending on whether they are right in front of you or on the phone. I wanted to see how these candidates responded when the client wasn't right in front of them.

Candidates who progressed beyond the group interview were invited to do a phone role play. We gave the candidates an abbreviated version of our phone script and asked them to run through some role plays with us over the phone. This gave us the chance to offer some coaching on how to improve their phone manner. Part of this was practical training, but it was also an instructive way of observing how the candidates reacted to feedback. Did they get defensive, or did they welcome the advice? This told us a lot about the candidates and what to expect from them as employees.

We were able to get a good sense of the candidate and the candidate was also able to acquire a much better sense of the job as well as the training they would receive.

Part of their interview was always a role play on the phone to get a sense of how they handled this part of the job, and how closely they could stay to our message. If you employ a lot of people who spend time working on phones, chances are you have some sort of script for them to follow. This way, you can make sure that all your employees are sending the same message to customers. You have also, most likely, refined your script to make the pitch more effective. Your employees need to understand this.

The phone role play was important for several reasons. First, we got to see if the candidate could stay on script. A surprising number of candidates get thrown when talking on the phone, and they end up changing the script to make it easier for *them*.

The other reason the phone role play was so revealing was that it showed how candidates responded to our feedback. At the beginning of the exercise, we would give the candidate a copy of the script and let them read it over. They could then ask us any questions they had about the script. Then we'd do a little coaching on how to make the script as appealing as possible. Finally, we'd run through the role play to see how the candidate performed.

Typically, candidates tried to do as good a job as possible, but we never expected them to do everything perfectly on the first try. This was a major opportunity for us to see how they reacted to feedback. Once we had done the role play, we'd do a little coaching before trying the role play again. This allowed me to see if they had taken the advice to heart and made an improvement. But it also allowed me to see how well the candidate handled the feedback. Were they open to hearing feedback so they could improve, or did they bristle at my advice? If they became defensive or simply didn't want to hear any feedback at all, I knew that this candidate wasn't the right fit.

I've had so many employers tell me that they don't expect new hires to be perfect. But what they do expect is that their new hires will be coachable. Doing the phone role play as part of the interview allowed me to gauge just how coachable these candidates would be. But we also wanted to make sure they had the right manner on the phone.

When you've done all the initial screening, and you've chosen some final candidates, how do you know what to ask them when they come in for their one-on-one interview? This, it turned out, was something most employers had no idea about. As a result, they tended to repeat questions they had heard at interviews. But I wanted to know how to craft powerful interview questions; the kind that would allow me to see what I needed to see.

*How to craft effective interview questions*

Candidates have likely heard the same interview questions over and over. What are your strengths? What are your weaknesses? Can you describe a time that you were challenged at a job and overcame that challenge? These are standard, boilerplate questions, and most candidates already have an answer in mind for these questions. These answers are usually well thought out versions of what the candidate thinks the interviewer wants to hear. But does this really tell you what you need to know about this person? Do these questions pertain to your company culture and mission? And if you're only getting rehearsed answers, are you really learning anything new?

Interviews are difficult because both parties want something, and this can lead to a certain amount of confusion or outright deception. I've had CEOs come to me and say that they hired a new employee who just seemed to check all the boxes. Great personality, great experience, great fit for the culture, but then after they're hired, they're not that person at all. I've had employers say to me, "This is not at all the person I interviewed."

The problem is you might not be asking the right questions. This part of the process is often overlooked by employers because they don't think about how to ask questions during an interview. Often, they don't even have a set list of questions but rather shoot from the hip, and this doesn't always tell them what they need to know. When I start working with a new client, I try to guide them to what they should ask, and what they should listen for in the answer.

Traditionally, interviewing has been a directive process where the interviewer asks direct questions to the candidate. The problem with this is that people are naturally nervous when they go to job interviews. So, all this process really shows you is who is good at interviewing. Not surprisingly, this has very little to do with who will be a good employee. I've interviewed people who were charming and charismatic without a hint of anxiety, and they were terrible employees. They were just good at interviewing.

The more modern approach to interviewing is to help your candidates feel comfortable so they can let their guard down a bit. Ideally, the interview should feel like a conversation rather than an interrogation, and you want the candidate to feel as though they have some control over the situation, even if they don't.

The goal of this style is honesty. The more relaxed someone is, the more their guard is down, the more likely they are to answer your questions openly and honestly. I'm not implying that people lie intentionally when their defenses are up, but they will tend to try to protect themselves. This can lead to the candidate being much more careful about how they answer a question. This doesn't necessarily mean that they will just start telling lies, but it does mean that they might answer a question in a way that doesn't really give you all the information that you need. Keep in mind, the interview is chiefly about you learning about this person. If they are nervous and you can't get them to open up, you won't know if this is the right person for you.

We start most of our interview questions with the phrase, "*Could you...?*" This is less directive and helps the candidate feel like they have an element of control. It is also more conversational. The candidate will feel less like they are being told what to do and more like you want to get to know them. It is subtle, but it works

Now that we helped the candidate to feel more relaxed, we want to learn about their specific experiences that may serve them well in our position. When I interview someone, I want to find out how this person handled work challenges in the past; concrete examples of what they did in a particular situation.

Prior to the interview, think about the kinds of situations that have come up at your business regularly. Then, craft questions around it. For example, *"Could you share a SPECIFIC EXAMPLE of a time you were asked to perform a task or accomplish a goal where the instructions you received were not clear?"* This question may be a good one to ask if your work environment is a bit fast-paced and sometimes team members are asked to complete tasks without much direction. Another example, *"Could you describe a SPECIFIC time when you were asked to complete a difficult task or project at work, and everything seemed against you?"* This is a good question to get a feel for how proactive someone is and if they feel like they have control over their life or blame everyone else for their problems.

These types of questions get to the heart of how this person will handle challenges when they come along. If you are interviewing for a customer service position, ask about a time when the candidate had to deal with a difficult customer. But don't ask them how they resolved it. This gives away the whole game. As the interviewer, you don't know if they were able to successfully resolve the situation, but if you ask them to describe the whole situation, it leaves room for the candidate to tell you a story about what they did or did not do.

A candidate who has addressed this type of situation in the past and was able to resolve the situation will be able to explain what happened in detail. They may also share with you what they learned from the situation, and how this has affected their behavior going forward. As an interviewer, I'm more concerned with an employee learning and growing than I am with them just putting out a fire and moving on.

On the other side of the spectrum are the candidates who start to picture a difficult customer in a negative way. Often, these candidates will tell you about an interaction with a difficult customer, but there is no resolution. It's simply a sob story about a time they were mistreated by a customer and managed to come out ok on the other side. That's not a resolution, and it tells me this person would not address a customer service issue the way I would want them to at my business. These people can identify a problem, but they never get to the solution. If they do, it will most likely involve a series of complaints about the customer followed by calling their manager to handle things. This is not the kind of person you want to hire because they lack the self-awareness to even understand that you want them to demonstrate certain basic qualities like self-reliance and leadership.

One of the problems I see too often is hiring managers wanting the candidate to succeed to the point where they can't resist helping a bit. This is natural, but it doesn't get you to your objective: hiring the right people. This also goes back to what I mentioned earlier about hiring managers or business owners who fall in love with candidates during the interview to the point where they overlook important details. If you like the person that you are interviewing, you will want them to succeed at the interview, and this may cause you to give the candidate help with the questions. This is a mistake for two reasons:

First, you are not challenging the candidate enough to know if they will be a good employee, but you're also giving them preference simply because you like their personality. Not only will you be taking a chance on someone, but you are also acting unfairly towards your other candidates.

When I look at candidates, what I want to see is control. Does it feel as though the candidate has control over the situation, or do they just complain about problems they've faced in the past. Do they seem more focused on solutions or problems? Can they be specific when asked, or do they tend to stick to generalities?

I try to ask for very specific examples when I interview candidates because I want them to be able to give me the details of a problematic situation and the details of how they dealt with it. I don't want to hear that a customer was "difficult" or "demanding," I want to hear what that customer said or did that was difficult or demanding. And I want to know what, specifically, this candidate did to resolve the situation. The context is very important.

When I coach business owners, I ask them to consider the whole story, not just the conflict. How did this difficult situation arise? What were the steps taken to resolve it? What did the candidate learn for future interactions? A good candidate will see this question coming, and they should have a good and complete answer prepared. If you ask for this information and the candidate won't commit to any hard details, something is wrong. Afterall, it is very difficult to lie in details.

The next thing I'm concerned about in their answer is actions. What are the specific actions the candidate took? This is another area where unprepared or unqualified candidates revert to speaking in generalities. This is where it's important to keep following up on answers. We call this probing. One easy way to do this is to ask what happened next or to ask them to walk you through what happened, step-by-step. What specific actions did the candidate take? Don't settle for "we did...." Let them know that this is an interview, and you want to know the specific actions that they took in this situation.

I frequently hear the word "we" at this point in interviews. "We" is a great way to obfuscate one's role in a situation because it's vague and noncommittal. I also understand that people tend to defer to the royal we in these situations because we're taught that teamwork is valuable. When I coach business owners, I try to make a point of this because it's something we often don't think about. I want the interviewer to watch out for the use of "we" in interviews so they can push back against it.

Ideally, I want interviewers to express to the candidate that they appreciate the fact that they have a team outlook, but I want to know the actions they took. I always want to know exactly what *this* person was doing during the encounter. If it turns out they just called a manager to solve the problem, their role is less significant, and I want to know that.

If I find that a candidate is using the word "we" a lot, I tell them once, and only once, that they have permission to just talk about themselves and their actions. Good candidates will see this as a sign that they can brag about themselves a bit, and they will start to go into exactly what they did. They will also be specific about the results of their actions and what happened next.

It's important to keep in mind that interviewing is a skill on both sides. Typically, candidates have had a lot of practice interviewing, and they know what the interviewer is looking for. This might sound like they're gaming the system, but they're not. They know that they are in competition with other people who are also qualified for this job. If you have five candidates who all have equivalent experience and skill levels, how do you choose one? More often than not, you're going to choose the one who performs the best in their interview.

On the other side of the equation, you need to have the right strategy and practice that strategy in order to be a good interviewer. If you are asking the right questions, and you follow up to get the details, you will find that each interview you conduct gets better. As a result, you will start to feel more comfortable about the process. But here's the thing—you need to have a process.

As with anything we do, interviewing requires practice. If you are interviewing with a process for the first time, you might find that you aren't happy with the results, and you might be wondering what you did wrong. The answer is: nothing. As with most skills, we need frequent practice and feedback in order to understand what we're doing right and wrong. But if you stick with it, you will get better at it.

I was recently working with a new recruiter, and we conducted an interview together for a sales position. Afterwards, I asked the recruiter what she thought about the candidate. She responded that she thought he was a very strong candidate, so I asked her why she thought that.

She said that the candidate presented himself well, was well dressed and seemed confident. So, I said, "Really?" At first, it was clear that the recruiter felt as though she had missed something important.

"What, specifically, did he say that was so impressive?" I asked. "What did he say that made you feel as though he knew what he was talking about?"

She thought about this for a moment, but she couldn't think of anything.

"I've done a lot of interviews for sales positions," I said, "and this guy seemed to have really good self-esteem, but he didn't say anything specific about his process. He didn't tell us how he fills his pipeline, or how he generates his leads or how he closes the leads he has."

I could tell that the recruiter was responding more to the candidate's presentation and manner than to what he had said. "If a candidate has a good process for sales, they're going to want to tell you all about it. They're not going to avoid those specifics."

After we had interviewed a few more candidates, the recruiter started to see what I was talking about. There are plenty of people out there who are good at the rapport building part of the interview, but there are far fewer candidates who can back that up with solid skills. After a short time, the recruiter was able to tell the difference, and this helped her to refine her process for interviewing. It showed her what to pay attention to and what to question.

Life is messy and work-life is no different. We all have obstacles we come across at work on a fairly regular basis. A successful employee will be one that believes he/she can overcome obstacles and wants to.

The only way to start to predict how a prospective employee will approach and handle those challenging situations is to find out how that person has handled similar situations in the past.

- Does he/she seek out a solution or does he/she believe the situation is impossible?
- Does he/she learn from the experience and therefore is better prepared for the future, or does he/she quit too soon?

While there are many other points to consider when creating your interview questions, crafting questions that garner a response from a candidate that helps you answer the above two questions is paramount.

Keep in mind:

- A success-oriented person will speak in SPECIFIC details about the situation, the actions they took and the results.
- A person who feels they don't have control over their results will blame others for the situation or speak in generalities.

Follow this formula when crafting an interview question:

1. "Could you share..."
   - Use this phrasing to help relax the candidate and give them the feeling of an element of control.

2. "a SPECIFIC example..."
   - Using the word SPECIFIC is powerful. You want details. This is how you get it.

3. "of...<insert a common situation you run into at your place of work>?"
   - Use a common work challenge you see at your business. Don't make it so specific to your particular business that the candidate cannot answer it but relate it enough that you see how the candidate has behaved in similar situations in the past.

4. Leave it hanging.
   - Don't follow up with, "How did you resolve the situation?" See what they share with you. If you need to follow up to get more details, refer to our Probing Questions in the Dream Team portal on how to do this. One easy way to do this is to ask what happened next or to ask them to walk you through what happened, step-by-step.

*Conducting the interview*

Conducting an interview is a skill that needs to be practiced. Below are some tips to help you get started on conducting effective interviews.

1. Be PREPARED
    - Review the job posting and what results you expect from a successful person in this position. Know this BEFORE you interview your first candidate.
    - Review all information you have from the candidate up to this point.
    - Make sure you've written out and practiced the questions you plan to ask.

2. Be ON TIME
    - Show the candidate respect from the start by being on time and ready for them. You will also be role modeling what you will expect from them if they are hired.

3. Be FRIENDLY and SMILE
    - Help the candidate to relax. You don't want this to be a painful experience for either of you. It will make you look bad and bring up the defenses of the candidate.

4. DON'T SHOW ANY JUDGEMENT
    - If you don't agree with a response, try not to show it. Keep the rapport positive throughout. Help the candidate feel safe to share with you.

5. Let the CANDIDATE DO MOST OF THE TALKING
    - When you are talking, you are not learning about the candidate and are wasting valuable time.

## MOST OF ALL...BE CURIOUS!

One of the biggest interviewing mistakes we see employers make is accepting all interview responses as they are delivered. I always say, *"Be curious!"*

If you receive a response that does not give you a complete picture, then you need to learn more. Complete responses will tell you – C.A.R.

- **C**ontext: The setting or backstory of the situation s/he is describing.
- **A**ctions: The candidate's role and the actions s/he took.
- **R**esults: The result of the candidate's actions – good or bad as well as what they learned.

Asking questions as described in the previous section doesn't always get you all of the information you need from the candidate. This is why we recommend using a technique called probing, or follow-up questioning. **Check out our Probing Questions That Work in the Dream Team portal for examples you can use.**

## DON'T JUMP TO CONCLUSIONS OR MAKE ASSUMPTIONS

Make sure you don't jump to conclusions – good or bad about the candidate's response. Going on gut or intuition may not get you the results you want and need. Always keep in mind that the candidate in front of you may have a different perspective than you. If the candidate says, "I always go above and beyond for my clients," to them that may mean s/he smiles and is respectful. You may be thinking it means that if s/he doesn't know the answer, s/he will research it and follow up with the client. If you don't ask more questions to learn how the candidate acted in the past, you won't have a good idea of how s/he will act as a member of your team.

## STILL NOT SURE WHEN TO PROBE (ASK FOLLOW-UP QUESTIONS)?

Listen for the candidate's use of hypotheticals like "We" or "You should...." The use of phrases like these indicates that the candidate is speaking in generalities and is not sharing with you specific actions s/he took in the past. Your goal is to hear statements that start with, "I did...."

## GAIN CLARIFICATION

Probing questions are also good to gain clarification. The candidate may be nervous and forget to include important details. Follow-up questions help you to bring out of the candidate a more complete picture. This will help you to determine if s/he has the competencies needed for your position.

You may also pick up on inconsistencies in the response. Don't let those go by without questioning further. If something doesn't make sense, ask for clarification. It is ok to challenge the candidate to make sure you understand correctly.

## DON'T GIVE AWAY THE ANSWER

Another mistake I often see during interviews is that the interviewer gives away the answer. This often happens when they ask follow-up questions. How do they give away the answer? They ask follow-up questions like, "How did you fix that problem?" or "What did you do to make sure the customer walked away happy?" These questions are telling the candidate exactly what you want to hear. You want to see if the candidate tells you how s/he resolved the situation without you leading him/her to it. It will be the difference between hiring a person who complains about problems or a person who solves problems.

## "THE DEVIL IS IN THE DETAILS." MAKE SURE TO GET THEM.

You've put out the posting, you collected resumés, and you've done the interviews. What next? Now you must assess your candidates based on the information you have. This is the step I call the pre-hire assessment. This is when you get to take everything you've learned so far and evaluate it against what your position requires. In order to successfully hire a new employee, you need to make sure you've chosen the right person *before* you hire them. So, let's talk a little about how to narrow down the field so that you can choose the best possible candidate.

*Scoring your candidates*

LISTEN TO THE CANDIDATE'S RESPONSES. HOW DID THEY ACT IN PAST SITUATIONS? IS THAT HOW YOU WOULD WANT THEM TO BEHAVE IN YOUR ROLE AND COMPANY?

When scoring a candidate interview, keep these tips in mind.

- Don't judge a candidate early in the interview. We are looking for trends or patterns in the responses. A poor response to one question should not automatically rule out a candidate. Continue to listen to the candidate's responses objectively.
- Base your ratings on the specific information you gain from the candidate's responses. Do not go on gut or feelings.
- Make sure you get your CAR as described earlier for each example shared. This is the information you need to rate each response.
    - Context — The background of the situation
    - Actions — The actions the candidate took.
    - Results — The impact or results of the candidate's actions as well as what the candidate learned.

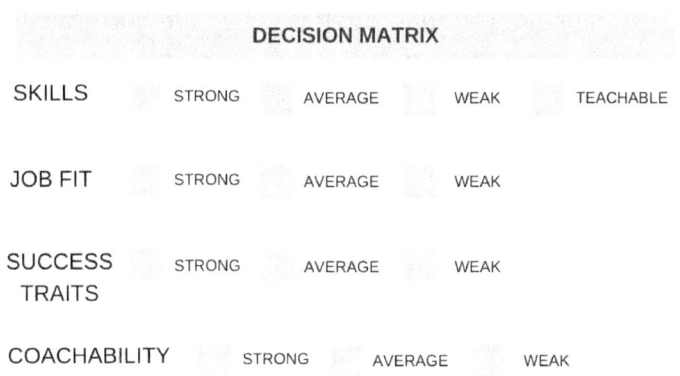

| | DECISION MATRIX | | | |
|---|---|---|---|---|
| SKILLS | STRONG | AVERAGE | WEAK | TEACHABLE |
| JOB FIT | STRONG | AVERAGE | WEAK | |
| SUCCESS TRAITS | STRONG | AVERAGE | WEAK | |
| COACHABILITY | STRONG | AVERAGE | WEAK | |

## HOW TO USE THE DECISION MATRIX

The picture above is the Decision Matrix we often use in our interview guides. Below, you will find brief descriptions of how to use each rating scale.

1. Skills - As experts in your industry, you will recognize responses that tell you this candidate knows how to do the job you need to be done. You will notice that we also included a "Teachable" option. If you find a candidate is teachable, but it not quite where you need them to be in skills, you may still decide they are a good hire for your position. However, if you are not prepared to provide them with training, then you are only setting them up for failure.
2. Job Fit - You will sometimes have candidates that have the skills to do the job, but the interest isn't there. When completing this rating, consider how this position fits into the candidate's career goals, what he or she enjoys doing and how passionate they are about your mission and core values.
3. Success Traits - These are the traits/characteristics that all your most successful team members in this or similar positions possess. They are the traits you know someone needs to have to do the job the way you want it done. Review the candidate's responses to your SPECIFIC EXAMPLE questions. Did you get all the details you needed through CAR? You may want to rate first each Success Trait individually — strong, average, or weak. If 75% or more are rated as strong, then rate this overall section as strong.

4. Coachability - Are they coachable? What did they say their previous supervisors will share as their area of improvement? If they don't know what any of their past supervisors felt they needed to improve, then their coachability is weak. If they shared SPECIFIC areas of improvement and what they are doing to improve in this area, then they are coachable. Visit the Dream Team portal for the Must ASK Questions that will help you to determine how coachable they are.

*Using pre-hire assessments*

Employers use a lot of different types of assessments in the workplace, and they all have different objectives. A behavioral assessment shouldn't be confused with a personality assessment, but they do have certain things in common. A behavioral assessment typically pertains to the types of behaviors that occur in the workplace. This tends to be a more focused type of assessment because it focuses on the practical aspects of doing a particular job. Other assessments try to determine one's emotional intelligence or work ethic, and some employers are concerned with practical matters like competence. Does the employee have good knowledge of the industry? Do they have good verbal or mathematical skills? How are those skills applied to this person's position?

When you are trying to figure out what kind of assessment is right for your situation, you first need to ask yourself what you want to accomplish with the assessment. If you are primarily concerned with measuring a candidate's specific skills and cognitive ability, you need to find an assessment that focuses on that. The other thing to consider is that these different assessments often work in concert to give you a fuller picture of your workforce. I often see employers relying just on a behavioral assessment, but that only tells you about one part of doing the job. To get an accurate prediction of how successful an employee will be, you need to take in more factors than a person's baseline behavior. What do I mean by this?

We all have our default setting. This is our comfort zone, and it's our preferred way of acting. But we also know that we all have the ability to move out of our comfort zone to be more successful. When considering candidates, we have to take this into account because we can end up passing on a talented candidate simply because their default setting isn't what you think will be successful in the workplace. Therefore, it's important to make sure you are using the right assessment, but you also need to consider *how* you are using the assessment.

Once you've identified the type of assessment you plan to use, make sure you administer it consistently and accurately. Take the time to learn how to correctly use the assessment.

The other thing I often stress is that assessments aren't foolproof. An assessment isn't a crystal ball. It's a communication tool that can teach you a great deal if you use it correctly, but you should never approach an assessment as if it was written in stone.

One of the red flags I see too often is employers relying too heavily on pre-hire assessments. It's important to keep in mind that assessments are just one tool to help you evaluate a candidate. I've even seen employers who require an assessment to be completed when a resume is submitted. If that candidate doesn't score high enough on the assessment, their whole application gets thrown out. In my opinion, this is a huge mistake because you can end up missing out on talented candidates simply because of one piece of the equation.

Some assessments can have a hidden bias that affects how candidates perform. Some candidates simply don't perform well on that kind of test. We all know someone of high intelligence who had trouble with the SATs. For this reason, I don't recommend using a pre-hire assessment until you have narrowed the field down to your final candidates.

Requiring candidates to complete an assessment at the beginning of the recruitment process could lower the number of applicants you receive. Look at this from the point of view of the candidate. Chances are that your job isn't the only one they are considering. At this point in the process, they don't have any reason to believe that they will be hired by you. They have no idea how many people are applying for your job. You have made no commitment to them, but now you've asked them to commit time to complete an assessment. Many employers think that this is a good way to weed out the candidates who aren't serious about the job, but in my experience, you end up losing out on talented people.

Once you've invested some time in your candidates, you can feel more comfortable about asking them to take the assessment because you've established some interest in them. When they sent in their resume, they signaled that they are interested in the job. To keep them interested, you need to create a give and take to show that you are serious about them as well. Once you've done this, candidates become much more inclined to take the assessment.

It's also important to stress the fact that an assessment is not a single determining factor. You need to explain that the assessment is merely another tool to get to know the candidates. As an employer, your goal is to find the right person for your position and culture. To do this, you need to know as much as possible about your candidates. This is what a pre-hire assessment should be. It's not a contest where there is a winner or loser. It's simply a tool to give you a better understanding of who will be successful in the job.

Whether you are doing pre-hire assessments or performance assessments after you've hired someone, it's important to make it clear that no assessment is a contest. There should never be the sense that a candidate might not be hired simply because of an assessment, and an employee should never feel as though a single assessment is the difference between getting promoted or fired. Why? Well, people get anxious. When most people get anxious, they don't perform as well. Even the most competent people get nervous, and therefore we can't rely on single tests to tell us everything we need to know.

It's also important to stress that an assessment isn't necessarily about answering questions correctly or incorrectly. In a trivia game, we know that there is an objectively correct answer to each question, but the questions on an assessment aren't usually structured that way. Again, the assessment is meant to be a communication tool, not a trivia game. Instead of right or wrong answers, the results of an assessment are merely a reflection of the person taking the assessment. This isn't about uncovering deep, dark secrets, and it's not intended to lead to a final decision. We're just trying to get a better sense of the person and their values.

When you are trying to figure out what kind of assessment is right for your situation, you first need to ask yourself what you want to accomplish with the assessment. If you are primarily concerned with measuring a candidate's specific skills and cognitive ability, you need to find an assessment that focuses on that. The other thing to consider is that these different assessments often work in concert to give you a fuller picture of your workforce. I often see employers relying just on a behavioral assessment, but that only tells you about one part of doing the job. To get an accurate prediction of how successful an employee will be, you need to take in more factors than a person's baseline behavior. Here are some things to consider when selecting and using a pre-hire assessment.

1. Make sure that the assessment that you're using is based on a body of research and theory that you know is highly regarded and that you believe is a good solid theory that you can wrap your head around. Typically, it's good to look at the company that's developing the assessment as well. See if they continue to research and validate their product.
2. Confirm that the assessment is validated against the job you are filling. A validated pre-hire assessment is one that is going to test competence, behavior and interest level for that position. You are scoring it against the needs for the job.
3. Use the results as a communication tool. An assessment is only as good as the conversation it creates. A good pre-hire assessment report will suggest interview questions to ask the candidate, so you can dig deeper. It may even suggest what to listen for from the candidate and how to probe.

4. Get training and support to ensure you are interpreting the assessment results correctly. There are many amazing coaches and consultants who took the time to get certified in different assessments. Don't go it alone.

If you decide to use the pre-hire assessment as part of your decision process in hiring, make sure you do your research first and don't rely on the assessment results alone to make your decision.

**CHAPTER 4**

# MAKING THE OFFER

*How to decide between two equally strong candidates*

Consider this: You've just gone through the process that we outlined in chapters one through three of this book. You've narrowed your field down, and then you winnowed it down some more. Finally, you're at the point where you have two candidates, and there's just one problem: They both seem to be a good fit for the job.

In a perfect world, there would be one perfect candidate who emerges from the pack and is clearly the best suited for the job. Of course, the worst-case scenario is that you go through the hiring process, and no one meets your standards. But let's not dwell on that now.

For now, let's concentrate on the possibility that you have two candidates who both appear to be equally qualified and suited to the job. What now? As I mentioned earlier in the book, I have worked with a lot of employers who fall in love with the first candidate who meets the qualifications. Employers will often want to rush into hiring these candidates partly because they don't want a good employee to slip through their fingers. What I try to explain to the employers that I work with is that there are plenty of fish in the sea, and it's perfectly fine to take a closer look at a candidate and maybe even pass on them.

Often, employers will find a candidate who appears to be exactly what they're looking for, so they ignore some key factors. What if a candidate has the right credentials, but in their interview, it becomes clear that they're looking to advance faster than you anticipate them advancing? This can create a situation where you hire a good employee only to lose them after a short time because they moved on to another opportunity that will give them the advancement they were always looking for.

It's important to understand that both the employer and the employee have their own motivations and goals. This is fine if both parties are aware of this, and if the motivations and goals don't conflict. Ask yourself who will be the best fit for your business and culture. Then, ask yourself who is going to fit best with where you want your business to go in the future.

About a year ago, I started working with a small company who had mostly been working with independent contractors, but the CEO wanted to hire a full-time W2 employee to be the operations manager. The CEO wanted to get out of the day-to-day work of operations and instead focus on growing the company.

After working with her to narrow down the qualities she was looking for in an operations manager, we ended up with a few good candidates. Then came the process of figuring out which of these good candidates she should hire. The candidates all had proven experience in operations, and from that standpoint, all of them seemed equally qualified. As we looked closer at the applicants, we realized that one of them had a background in marketing.

During the interview for this candidate, the CEO made a point of asking about her marketing experience and how that experience might be valuable to the future of the company. It turned out that the candidate had some ideas for her business in that area.

This is why it's important to have an understanding of where your business is going. If you are only looking in one narrow direction, you might miss talent and skills that you should have been looking for. In this situation, the CEO started to think that this candidate would perform well in an operations capacity, but in the future, she might be able to transition to a position that was more marketing oriented, and they could hire someone else to run operations. This is what set this candidate apart from the rest. She had something else to offer that the other qualified candidates did not. But you only find out about these things if you bother to look.

The company ended up being extremely happy with their new hire, and now they're in a position where they are looking to bring on another hire to be the operations manager's assistant so that the operations manager can start to focus more on marketing.

The problem I see too often with hiring is that employers are only looking to solve the problem in front of them today, rather than thinking about where they want to be in a year or five years. Being short-staffed is stressful for any business, but we always need to look at hiring as a process that isn't just about filling a current opening. Hiring should always be an opportunity to grow and evolve, but you need to know how to spot the right people to do that.

Most employees don't want to do the same job forever. We often think of this as climbing a ladder, but it's more complicated than that. Instead of just moving upward, employees often want to move laterally as well. Employees like to be challenged with new jobs that will allow them to learn new skills.

In the case of the company hiring the operations manager, they were able to find someone who fit their current need, but they also found someone who was looking to use their skills in a completely different capacity. This type of structure allows you to attract employees who have an incentive to stay with you.

If an employee takes a job with you, they might not stay if they don't have opportunities to grow their skillset and shift their focus. That employee will likely start to look for a job elsewhere so they can work in a different capacity. If you want to build a lasting team that will grow with you over the long term, you must consider what you offer your employees.

There is a give and take that constantly exists between employers and employees, and the only way that give and take can work properly is if both parties are happy with the arrangement. An employer satisfies an immediate need for the employee by giving them a job. Giving the employee the job satisfies an immediate need for the employer by filling an open role. But over time, the needs of the employer and the employee will change.

The employee will want to branch out and learn different skills, but if this isn't a possibility, they will look for another job. The employer wants to attract employees who will stay long term because that is easier than hiring and training new employees. They also want employees with a proven track record of trustworthiness so they can be given new responsibilities. This is a lot of give and take, and so far, none of it has to do with money. Obviously, employees will want to make more money as they work with the company, but that usually isn't what keeps them from leaving.

So, when it comes to two seemingly equal candidates, do you want to hire the one who will fulfill the needs of the current position and nothing else, or do you want to hire the one who can do that but has other skills as well? This one relationship isn't about the entire future of the company, and it isn't simply about the personal growth of the employee. It's about finding the person that you connect with who will want to be a part of your organization and will be happy in the long term.

I have experienced this in my own business as well. My business has grown significantly in the last couple of years, and this necessitated hiring full-time employees. As I've mentioned, I've been in the position to hire employees for other businesses that I've run, but this was the first time I was hiring a W2 employee for my recruiting business.

I needed a recruiter, and one candidate stood out to me the most. She had the right background and identified with our core values, but what really stood out to me was the fact that she made it abundantly clear that she was looking to grow. At this point, I had already decided to hire her, but the fact that she was insistent about growing within the company was what allowed her to negotiate during the offer process.

I offered her one rate, and this was when she made her case. She wanted a higher rate, but she was willing to offer something in return. She didn't want to be a recruiter for the rest of her life. She had already been doing that for a few years, and she envisioned herself transitioning to other areas of human resources, but she needed the opportunity to learn about these areas on the job. What impressed me about this candidate was that she was very clear about what she wanted and what she could offer. So, I agreed to a higher rate, but I knew that this was mostly a token. What she really wanted was a promise that she wouldn't be stuck in recruiting forever. So, I promised her that we would start offering her other opportunities in HR so that she could learn the skills she wanted to learn.

Because the business has continued to grow as a result of her efforts, I have been able to offer her the opportunities that she wanted. This is the kind of relationship that lasts. When a relationship is equitable and both parties get what they need, the relationship will continue. It's only when the relationship becomes one-sided that problems start to arise. This is when employers feel as though their employees aren't giving 100%, and employees feel as though their employer doesn't care about their well-being.

Ultimately, the goal is to find people whose talents and goals match up with what you want your business to do in the long term. When I was looking to hire a recruiter, I could have chosen someone who was fine with the idea of being a recruiter for the next five years, and I had candidates like that, but I wanted to hire someone who wanted to move up and fill a different spot in the future.

This is how we build real, lasting relationships within the workplace. As difficult as hiring can be, retention can be a challenge as well. We need to understand what makes an employee want to stay with you for the long term, but the mistake we often make is treating all employees the same.

We need to understand that every employee has different values in terms of what keeps them in their jobs. With some employees, it's simple: They want as high a salary as possible, and they want to see that salary continue to rise. But a surprising number of employees care about things other than their bottom line. These days, I see more and more employees who are chiefly concerned with professional development. These employees are less concerned with their current pay rate than with learning and developing new skills that will allow them to broaden and deepen their expertise so they can eventually move on to a different role within the company or at another company.

When I was hiring a recruiter, I was most impressed with the fact that my choice of candidate wanted to keep learning new things. This required me to provide her with additional resources, but I saw it as an investment rather than simply an expense. My goal, when hiring, is to zero in on what this individual employee values about their job and how I can support them.

*Negotiating the offer*

Most candidates will be aware that they have something to bring to the table, and they have an idea in their head about what that talent is worth. This is when it's important to know how to properly negotiate with a potential employee. You may not be able to give them everything they want, but you also don't want to scare them off.

There is an art to negotiations, and it's important to remember that it's not all about money. That said, money is usually where the negotiations start. I'm a fan of Maslow's hierarchy of needs theory. Maslow represents his theory as a pyramid of needs that will be satisfied from bottom to top. At the base of the pyramid are the "deficiency needs," or the physiological and safety needs. This is the foundation for every person, and as an employer you need to understand that the deficiency needs must be satisfied before a person starts to satisfy the growth needs like development.

For example, if you have a candidate who needs to make $50,000 per year to satisfy their basic living requirements (rent/mortgage, bills, food, child-related expenses, and basic entertainment), offering them a job that pays $40,000 isn't going to satisfy this basic requirement.

When starting this process, you need to be aware that every candidate comes with their own situation. Everyone has certain requirements whether it's family or health issues or debt. Every candidate has a dollar figure in their head that represents the amount of money they need to make in order to be comfortable. This is the first hurdle in the process because unless you can meet this basic need, your new employee may always feel the deficit.

Once you move up the pyramid, though, the motivating factors are usually less about money. We find that negotiating is more about personal development and upward mobility. This is the part of the negotiation where we learn what is most important to the employee. The first stage is about getting to a baseline of acceptability in terms of salary, but what are the factors that will make a candidate want to join your company and stay there?

I've had a lot of employers ask me: What happens when the negotiation gets stuck in the money phase? What do I do if the candidate just keeps pushing back for more money? Well, the simple answer is that, if a candidate tries to push you past a dollar figure you can afford to pay, try to negotiate from a different angle. What about this opportunity is so exciting for them? How can you offer the candidate opportunity for growth and even more money in the future? Try to steer the conversation away from the money they will earn today and more towards what you can build together to get them where they want to be in the future. If you do that, and they can't see the possibilities, this might be the point where you move on. This situation probably isn't right for either of you.

Once you've made the offer, give the candidate some time to think it over. I've had clients tell me they made a candidate an offer on a Friday, and the candidate didn't say yes immediately. Instead, the candidate said they would like to take the weekend to think about it and respond on Monday. For some employers this is a confusing thing to hear. This person just spent all this time and effort to get this job, they got the offer they said they wanted and now they don't know if they want the job?

I've had employers ask me if they should just move on to another candidate when this happens, and I always tell them no. The fact that a candidate wants to take time to consider an offer is a good thing.

Think of it this way: If I offered you a bag of money with $50,000 in it, and I told you that you can have it, no strings attached, you would probably jump at that offer. But if I told you I was offering you a salary of $50,000 and it would require you to come to work every day, and it might also impact the lives of your family, you might want to think about it and talk to your family about the implications of this new situation. This level of consideration only increases as you rise in the ranks of a company. When someone starts a new job, it can cause a whole host of changes for that person's life, and those changes might not all be apparent when they're sitting across from you receiving your offer.

Because of this, I always tell employers that they should feel comfortable giving their candidates a couple of days or a weekend to consider the offer. Any longer than that, and you might have a problem.

One of the issues that employers often raise with me is the idea of leverage. Most people, when looking for a new job, will apply and interview at numerous companies to increase their odds of getting an offer. In some cases, this means a candidate might end up with more than one offer, and they may take this opportunity to use one offer to improve another offer.

If you survey applicants, they will likely tell you that when they have a variety of options open to them, there is one job that stands out as the one they want most. It might be the company itself, or the position, or the salary, but chances are, they have a favorite. That doesn't mean that this job will be the one that gives them the most lucrative offer.

Another issue that employers face when making an offer is the fear that they don't have the budget to make competitive offers when it comes to salary. Employers often feel as though money is the ultimate deciding factor for every candidate, and they just don't have the resources to compete with larger companies. The fear is they will never be able to attract the best talent if they can't pay the highest salary.

Obviously, salary is an important factor for your candidates, but it's not the only factor for many of them. Most candidates won't accept an offer that is far below what another company might pay, but there are a lot of incentives you can offer your candidates during the negotiation phase that might motivate them to accept your offer. Keep in mind that if you can cross that salary threshold where the candidate doesn't have to worry about their financial needs being met, there are other attractive things you can offer them.

Right now, the biggest incentive a company can offer is flexibility. Obviously, some jobs will allow for more flexibility than others, but over the last couple of years, we've learned that a lot of jobs can be a lot more flexible than we thought. The main reason we never knew this is because we never had to figure out a more flexible model. Technology has been steadily improving over the last twenty years, but for the most part, we never changed the way we structured work. Zoom wasn't invented during the pandemic. We just figured out how to use Zoom to compensate for the pandemic.

What we've learned along the way is that many of the jobs that have always been thought of as "office jobs" can easily be done from a remote location with no productivity loss. It's likely that employers have suspected that this was the case for a long time because of the integration of so many new pieces of technology, but it was always a gamble. What if we move the bulk of our operation to remote work and then our workers lose their motivation? What if they don't hit their deadlines anymore because they don't have the structure of the office?

These factors have largely kept businesses from pursuing more remote work despite the fact that remote work significantly cuts a business' overhead. The experiment just seemed a little too dangerous. But once we were forced to work remotely, we were forced to undertake this experiment, and not surprisingly, it worked. Productivity did not fall off, and it turns out that a lot of people really like not having to commute to work. But it's more than just this. Employees have always had trouble balancing life and work because work typically requires us to be in a building between these hours regardless of whether our work demands it.

What people have found is that between work meetings, they might have an hour of downtime that allows them to accomplish household tasks or errands. These were tasks that once occupied tired evenings and intruded into relaxing weekends, but now they don't have to. We've found a way to make our lives more balanced, and a lot of employees simply do not want to go back to the old model. This is a huge opportunity for you as an employer.

Typically, money has always been the biggest factor in hiring negotiations, and other perks of the job were far less attractive. But what we've found over the last couple of years is that many employees value flexibility as much as a little more money. As an employer, you have a real opportunity to make the lives of your employees better without having to offer more compensation.

This is something I have tried to do with my own business because I recognized the benefits both to my company and to my employees' lives. But part of achieving this is getting out of the old mindset that says employees will only work hard if you are standing over them cracking the whip. This involves trust between you and your team because you need to be confident that they will get their work done with less supervision, and they must value the situation enough that it motivates them to stay on task and be productive. If you can achieve this balance with your team, there is no real downside to making their jobs more flexible.

Of course, there are different levels of flexibility, and you can also use this in negotiations. Perhaps an employee wants to work fully remotely, but you aren't comfortable with never having them in the office. Many companies are now trying hybrid working situations that allow employees to work from home on some days of the week and come to the office for in-person meetings on certain days.

In my business, I look for all kinds of ways to make my employees' jobs more flexible, but this always requires trust. If an employee comes to me and says, "I really want to take Friday afternoons off, but don't worry, I can make up the work over the weekend," that is fine with me... as long as they get the work done over the weekend.

I've found that not all employees thrive under the same working conditions. Some workers feel much more confident getting to the office at 9:00 am and working at their desk until 5:00 pm. But other workers are more productive at night. Or they might have childcare obligations that force them to break up their work into pieces throughout the day. Either way, if the work gets done, the business doesn't suffer.

Ultimately, when it comes to getting those absolute best employees, we need to make a good offer. I've told many clients that you should never let a great employee walk away simply because there is a sticking point. Is it a flexible schedule? Is it a better health insurance package? Whatever it is, if you want to attract the best talent, you need to offer them the incentives that they care about.

Right now, we're in a situation where employees are in on the secret: Work can be more flexible, and employers have the ability to offer more incentives. Employees know they have more leverage because all they must do is look around. Companies across the world are finding ways to stay productive while bending over backwards to keep their employees happy.

So, we've talked about money and flexibility, but one of the things we haven't touched on yet when it comes to making an offer and negotiating is titles. To me, this is a silly topic because I really don't get hung up on titles. I don't think they're important, but what I came to realize is that a lot of people do.

After interviewing enough candidates, I started to realize how important a title was to a lot of people. It turns out a little prestige can go a long way in making an employee happy in their job, and this is often something that comes up in a negotiation. In many cases, I've negotiated salary and benefits with a candidate, and it feels like we're almost there, but something is still missing. There's some factor that is keeping the candidate from accepting the terms, and often the candidate will say something along the lines of: "Everything with the offer looks fine but... can we just change my title?"

For me, this isn't a big deal. If you do the job well, and a different title makes you happy, let's figure out what title you'd like. Why does this matter to people, you might be thinking? Humans are naturally predisposed to the concept of hierarchy. We've always had leaders and a structure for our societies, and we have a need to know where we fit within this structure. We need to feel as though we have enough status within the structure, and this status makes us feel good. It's the same with status symbols. Some people might drive a high-performance luxury car because they have a deep understanding of and appreciation for how cars work, and this level of performance give them joy. But most people drive high-performance luxury cars because it is a symbol that you have a certain status within society. That person might be just as happy driving a less expensive car, but that car doesn't send a message to everyone else. It's really the same with titles. Having a prestigious title on your business card sends the message that you are important, and this is important to a lot of people.

If you find yourself fretting about whether to give in when titles become part of the negotiation, stop and ask yourself how important a title is to you. If you conclude that it's not really that important, but you really want this person as an employee, let them have the title they want if it still makes sense for the job.

You've written the perfect posting. You've cast a wide net to attract the best talent. You've refined your interview process, and you know what questions to ask, and what answers you wanted to hear. You've narrowed it down to a few great candidates and chosen the right one for the job. You negotiated an offer that works for both parties. Now what? It's time to make sure you properly onboard your new employee and set them on a path for success.

# CHAPTER 5

# ONBOARDING

They say you only get one chance to make a first impression. I don't think that's exactly true, but when it comes to onboarding, your job as an employer is to set your new hire up for success and make them feel welcome in their new position. This employee had a chance to make an impression on you, and you had an opportunity to make an impression on them. Both of you have decided that working together is a good idea, but now comes the part where you form that working relationship.

By the time your new employee shows up, you need to make it clear that you are ready for them to get started, and you can't wait for them to come aboard. This means that you've taken some steps to show your new employee that you've put in some work to prepare for their presence in the workplace. This might mean that you've put their nameplate on their office door or set up their new email address. You've gotten their logins and business cards ready for them.

Below is an excerpt from an onboarding checklist. To download the full checklist that outlines the first 90 days, log on to the Dream Team portal.

## TWO WEEKS PRIOR TO START DATE

*Goal: Make them feel welcome*

- Send an introduction email to your team and copy new hire.
- Send new hire company swag and a welcome video.
- Confirm start date and time

## ONE WEEK PRIOR TO START DATE

*Goal: Make them feel welcome*

- Prepare and send new hire welcome email, including...
  ◦ Date and time of arrival and who to ask for upon arrival
  ◦ What to bring, i.e., identity documents, contracts, etc.
  ◦ Dress code, lunch suggestions and FAQs for new hires
  ◦ Parking, office map and directions for how to enter your office
  ◦ Attach employee handbook and other policies (i.e., IT security policies)
  ◦ Schedule for first day — what to expect
  ◦ A list of the team and their roles

That first day is an important one. It's the day that will set the tone for every day that follows, so you want to make sure that you spend that day talking to your new employee much in the way that you talked to them during the hiring process. That was the part where you started to get to know them. Onboarding is the process where you continue to get to know them and help them to know you.

This is also a good time for reinforcement. Communicate your vision to them again. Tell them where you see the company going and, specifically, how their position fits into that vision. Part of doing this is communicating to your new hire what success means.

A good way to approach this subject is to create a performance scorecard. This can go back to the job description that you wrote when you created your job listing. What are the different results that this position is expected to achieve? You can also list some of the ways that this position specifically contributes to the overall mission of the company. One of the things that employees can struggle with, especially as time goes on, is how their efforts matter beyond meeting expectations and collecting a paycheck. People feel better in their jobs when they feel as though they are essential to the operation. Otherwise, they can come to feel as though their job isn't important, and their performance starts to slide as a result.

By revisiting the mission of the company, you can establish with your new employee how they fit and what is expected of them right out of the gate. This idea of revisiting the core mission is also something that should be reinforced regularly in team meetings, and you should be actively asking these questions: What is our mission? What is our purpose? What are our values? And also, what has changed and needs to be addressed?

Before a new hire starts work, make sure you've communicated to the rest of the team that a new team member is going to be joining the company so they can reach out and introduce themselves. The easiest way to do this is to send an email to all of your team members letting them know that a new person is going to be joining the team. Give everyone the new hire's email address in advance. Then encourage them to send the new employee a message welcoming them to the team and remind them to check in with the new employee on day one.

I had a new assistant start recently, and while I was training her on how to use Slack on her first day, other employees would chime in to say hello and welcome her to the team. One after another, the entire team took turns saying hello and introducing themselves, and my new assistant had a huge smile on her face the whole time. Within two minutes, she felt like she was a member of the team. We might think of these as small, insignificant things, but they matter so much on that first day.

We need to be conscious of the fact that starting a new job can be very intimidating. It's like starting at a new school where everyone already knows each other. But in the case of a new job, a new employee knows that they need to start operating as part of the team immediately. And you need to make sure that you are setting expectations for both your new employee and the rest of the team.

This is a good time to address how you will be communicating with the new employee and how you want them to communicate with you. By this point, you've already told them what results you expect, but you need to make sure that you are both on the same page when it comes to how to communicate.

Communication includes how feedback is delivered, and I realized that not all employees are receptive to feedback in the same manner. Sometimes with a new employee, I'll just ask them how they like to receive feedback. Do they like it in written form, or do they prefer it verbally? Also, how do they like to hear good or bad news? And I also like to get a sense of how and when they want to meet with me to check in about how things are going.

At the beginning of a job, some people want a lot of communication, but others don't. Some employees like to make sure you are aware of what they're doing at all times so you can give them a thumbs-up, and other employees like to take a little time to figure out the job without constant contact.

I find that the most important thing is to be very upfront about all of this. Even the simple stuff can feel daunting for a new employee at first. So, make sure they know where the bathroom is and the system for lunch breaks. These things are second nature to you and your other team members, but for a new hire, everything is new and different from their last job.

All of this is part of making a new employee feel welcome and comfortable. It might seem small, but it's important. There is a lot of stuff to accomplish when you onboard a new hire. Because of that, I like to have all of this planned out ahead of time, so the first two weeks run like an agenda. This period should be about training, setting expectations and making connections. The new hire should be attending meetings to get a sense of how the rest of the team interacts with each other. And you want to start including the new employee in some actual work so they can have some small successes right away. But this should be a gradual approach. You don't want your new employee to feel overwhelmed. The goal is to make them feel as though they are making contributions right away.

*Conducting a performance review*

I don't believe in tying performance reviews to compensation decisions. Instead, I believe performance feedback is most beneficial when it is given in the moment and based upon observable, measurable information. Feedback is also not useful unless it is shared with actionable steps to improve.

There are two goals to a performance review in the employee's mind. To learn:

1. What do you expect of me?
2. How am I doing at meeting your expectations?

Most people want to do a good job. They don't always know what you consider to be a good job. This could make them feel lost and unmotivated. Make sure to communicate and do check-ins with your team members often.

A solid performance review has two components:

1. Behavioral Focus – How I do my job. This includes the areas we discussed early on in this book. How does my

position contribute to the organizational mission? Am I living the organizational core values? Am I exhibiting the success traits we talked about that are important to be successful in the position?
2. Result Focus – What I have accomplished. Have I accomplished the goals – both qualitative and projects – that were expected of me?

Starting with these two components bring it back to how you communicated your expectations from the beginning – starting with the job posting. It keeps you on the same page, consistent and leaves less room for surprises.

Once you have your performance tool in place, approach the review and conversation with a forward-looking approach. You can't change the past, so it doesn't make sense to focus on what you cannot change. Instead, guide the conversation around the skills you want the employee to sharpen or develop and how the employee can add more value to the organization. Include how you plan to support them in these efforts. What resources can you provide them with? Ask them if there are other ways you can support them.

This approach gives the employee a sense that they have an opportunity to improve and grow rather than making them feel as though they are being shamed for actions they can't go back and change. Make sure your employees know that you appreciate the things they are doing well. This can be the foundation for motivating them to make the improvements they need to make.

So, what if you find yourself with an employee who just doesn't seem to be performing the way you want them to?

Let's say you've been through your training plan, you've given feedback and laid out the pathway to growth, but there's still something wrong. Throughout the hiring process, this person seemed like the right fit for you, but now you're facing the brutal reality that you may have made a mistake. This happens to everyone sooner or later, but you can right the ship if you take the correct actions.

First, make sure you document everything you do with this employee. You need to document the fact that you've done everything in your power to help this person succeed, and it still hasn't worked. Look carefully at your process to make sure that you really have done everything you can to help this person perform the job.

Sometimes, the problem with an employee is a matter of their attitude. It's entirely possible that they had a great attitude about *getting* the job, but they don't have such a great attitude when it comes to actually *doing* the job. If this is the case, it's probably time to let that person go so they can find a better fit for them.

If the problem with the employee is a matter of skill, and you feel as though you've done everything you can to help them be successful, it's probably in their best interest to let them go so they can find a place where they can be successful.

It's also important to try to identify why the problem is happening. Is this a fixable situation or not? I've found that some attitude problems can be temporary and can be based on factors that are not connected to the job. Perhaps your employee is having a conflict at home that is creeping into their performance at work. This is a situation where you can sit down with the employee and try to understand what they're dealing with so you can try to move forward. You may find that they're just having a bad day or a bad week, and this will pass.

The key is identifying and understanding what is going on. I don't like to sweep things under the rug, so when I'm dealing with an employee and something doesn't seem quite right with them, I want to find out what's going on. If this employee usually has a good attitude, but something is bothering them, it's important to me to know the root cause because otherwise the negative feelings can tend to metastasize like a cancer, and things will get progressively worse over time.

I've found that in these types of situations, just encouraging the employee to share what's going on releases them from the mood they're stuck in. People tend to respond very well to unburdening themselves, and often this will solve the problem. It might be something as simple as they haven't had a good night's sleep in a few days, and they're tired. Sometimes employees aren't even aware of how they show up.

Obviously, your job isn't your whole life, and as an employer, it's your job to understand that your employees live complicated and challenging lives in the hours when they aren't at work. If you have an employee who seems to be struggling with something, it's possible they aren't aware of the way they are perceived by others. Sometimes, just checking in with the team member to see if they are ok will change the behavior.

Make sure to always check with your legal counsel and HR advisor when addressing employee situations.

# CONCLUSION

Employees tend to come and go, and your business is an ever-evolving organism that you need to maintain. As soon as you feel as though you have the perfect team, one of them will decide they need to leave for whatever reason. If you follow the steps that I've laid out, you can avoid having your whole organization thrown into chaos when this happens. But at every stage of your business, you need to make sure that you are doing the work to maintain your workplace and culture so that you are free to grow and expand your business. Your employees are the backbone of your business, and to thrive, you need to identify and foster the right people in a healthy environment. My goal was to give you the right roadmap to get there.

# DREAM TEAM MEMBERSHIP PORTAL

Throughout this book, we mentioned additional resources that are available to you on our Dream Team Membership portal. This is FREE to you for 3 months from the first time you log in. Please use this link to set up your free account.

*http://www.joinaha.com/*

www.ingramcontent.com/pod-product-compliance
Lightning Source LLC
Chambersburg PA
CBHW052323220526
45472CB00001B/245